BLANCA BLANCO

810 Eastgate North Dr., Suite 200
Cincinnati, Ohio 45245
www.britonpublishing.com

ISBN 978-1-956216-01-1 Hardcover
ISBN 978-1-956216-05-9 Paperback

Briton Publishing, LLC books are distributed by Ingram Content Group and made available worldwide.

To my beautiful Mami, my siblings, my tias, my teachers who were always there for me, and to all who are motivated to succeed.

Table of Contents

Foreword

by Edward I. Byrnes, Ph.D.

Breaking the Mold
Professor of Social Work – Eastern Washington University

There are many good reasons to read this book. Blanca begins with her childhood, juxtaposing deep love with complex trauma and the ongoing indignities of poverty. She proves resilience to be more than a passive characteristic. Instead, resilience is an active and deliberate process here. Her story reflects many principles of Cognitive Behavioral Therapy (CBT), but what is most remarkable is how she understood and used such principles long before she learned them in college.

Her childhood effectively balances candor with calmness, taking us on a journey in which Blanca works to help her family as a high school student and achieves extraordinary academic performance in undergraduate and graduate school. Just as inspiring is how she developed the modeling and acting career in which she now excels. Our preconceptions about academic pursuits in psychology and social work might seem inconsistent with modeling and acting, but Blanca's story proves how imagination, which she cultivated from her early childhood forward, integrates with natural curiosity about human nature.

Sound self-guidance directly informs several chapters of this book. Breaking The Mold is not a clinical book, but those who are familiar with CBT will at once recognize its primacy in guiding her life. Goal and subgoal setting, successive approximation of behavioral goals, recognizing realistic versus unrealistic expectations and other cognitive distortions, re-framing and cognitive restructuring and the power of affirmation and positive thinking are all components in her success.

CBT practitioners will also readily recognize Blanca's plain language guidance for challenging limiting beliefs, behavior activation, maintaining health-promoting routines, and analog exposure therapy. Blanca independently developed many of these principles for herself as a child who was coping with trauma, poverty, and ostracism. Those obstacles were rooted in prejudice and racism, making CBT principles necessary long before she learned their technical names.

She integrates CBT principles in her ways of thinking and living rather than as isolated techniques. She recognizes emotions as temporary states, acknowledging how thoughts lead to actions and how re-framing becomes not simply a device for removing negative thoughts but also a path toward greater personal growth.

What is also unique is how she offers readers guidance by rooting it in her lived experience. Her guidance is never overly clinical or subjective, but instead, it directly speaks to readers by showing how she moves through challenges in a positive, healthy, and self-directed way.

Her skillful storytelling also adds value to this book. Blanca writes with candor about traumatic experiences, whether about her childhood of poverty, prejudice, and abuse or describing in vivid detail the Woolsey Fire she lived through. Experts and survivors agree that a necessary part of recovering from a traumatic event is telling your story – technically known as exposure. Clearly, unflinchingly, she exposes traumatic experiences to make them a form of therapy for her. Further, Blanca invites us to share in this process as her readers. She encourages anyone who has survived a traumatic event to take necessary steps to face the fear that allows trauma to take hold, and indeed to break trauma's mold.

Blanca is no stranger to extraordinary challenges and effort, we realize, nor is she a stranger to humility. She consistently credits the influence and examples of her mother, aunts, and grandmother, as well as those like me who have had the good fortune to serve her as mentors.

Blanca's story defies statistical odds. Young Latinas and women of all backgrounds will be inspired to imagine moving beyond their present circumstances, embracing goals, and recognizing daily progress as they persevere.

Her story here clearly proves that having odds against you always also means you have odds working for you. Through her story and guidance, we are all reminded of the strength and value that comes from being at our most present in everything we do.

Introduction

I wrote this book hoping it would motivate and inspire others. You will read all about the challenges and hardships my family and I had to endure to reach our goals.

Success is within reach for anyone if desire and determination are the driving force in achieving it. Taking small steps towards one's goals every day can be challenging but it is not impossible.

My book is not only about the bad things that can, and often will happen in our lives, but also it will show that life is not linear. It's filled with ups and downs like a rollercoaster. Some things are outside of our control, but as you will read here in my story, we have the power to change our own narrative and our own future for each of us to be successful. It is vital to understand that success will always be different for each of us; however, it is in the decision to at least try, which is often the most important first step.

You will read about our poverty, our determination, the strength our mother showed us and remains within us. She showed us how to overcome all that life threw at us she came up smiling and stronger every time.

My book will also show that at an early age I had to learn to turn barriers into challenges because doing so allowed me the opportunity to have control and to challenge myself to achieve my goals.

The strategy I have applied throughout my life has helped me to achieve the goals I set myself and I didn't want my circumstances, living in poverty, to define my future. So I took action to ensure I changed the trajectory of my life to one of success that I am proud of.

We came through having to uproot from our home in Mexico, learn a new language while overcoming the stigma of being an immigrant family, living in a garage without hot water and heat.

But, we did make it! Each of us. My siblings and I went to college and university. We all obtained degrees and became successful, as you can too.

I learned to take action tirelessly to defeat all the odds that were stacked against me while building my resiliency and an unstoppable determination. This was one of the many skills I learned at an early age and one of the many, I am sharing in my book.

Lastly, my story has a happy ending which I hope you will love, as I do, but no cheating, read it through and enjoy!

Chapter 1:

Life in Mexico

Life is either a daring adventure or nothing at all. — *Helen Keller*

I was born in Watsonville, California and when I was 3 years old, my family moved back to Mexico, because my father's mother was sick. Our home town was in Tecomán Colima, in the southwest of Mexico. Our neighborhood was middle class. The surrounding area was very beautiful, and I had my family and my friends close by.

I have 4 siblings, 2 brothers, and 2 sisters and I am the second oldest. We had a large extended family living close by. My siblings and I had lots of friends and cousins all around us. Life was, for the most part, good.

My father was a policeman in the Tecomán Colima Policía and served 30 years on the police force. Once when he was attempting to arrest a robber, he was shot in the ankle. He had to re-learn to walk but later was shot again in another incident. The second time, the bullet went through both of his legs. His recovery was slow and very painful as he had to learn to walk once again.

He was not always a loving man, sometimes he was an abusive father and husband. On some occasions, he could be a fun-loving father, but other times he would scare me and hit me with a "chicote" a type of switch or whip used to control horses. Other times, he would use his belt or a chancla (a type of shoe). He even held his gun to our mother's head and threatened to shoot her right in front of us. We were all scared of him, especially our mother. We were all crying and trying to protect our mother who he had pushed onto the bed. We surrounded her, begging him not to shoot. His rage and uncontrolled anger were all because she was asking him to give her money to buy us food when he suddenly snapped.

My mom used to pack dad's lunch for work every day and sometimes he would return home with ladies' underwear in his lunch box. It always caused an argument and we knew it would be another unhappy night at home. My dad was flirtatious and was known locally as a womanizer.

My mom was a hard worker and we could see that she suffered a lot during that time in Mexico with his bullying behavior directed not only to our mom but also toward us. There were other things she had to put up with that were going on at the time with his constant anger.

But the main reason for her decision was that she knew she could never make a complaint to the police about his aggressive behavior towards her and us, as they would never deal with "one of their own." So she made the choice to move us all to America where the laws would protect her and us all from dad's constant physical abuse.

Living in Tecomán Colima had become more dangerous than before for us and we knew there was a very real possibility that with my father's line of work, the odds were high that he may be shot again. He had dodged death twice, and we were very worried that he may not dodge a bullet a third time. Even though he was abusive, we still loved him and cared for his safety.

My maternal grandmother, who wanted us to leave Mexico as soon as possible, worked hard to scrape up enough money together to send enough money to my mom so we all could leave Mexico and move to the USA. It would be very expensive for us to make a fresh new start after we got to the U.S.

When the money finally arrived by wire from the USA to our local bank, mom was so excited and took me with her to withdraw the money. All went well at the bank and we withdrew the money in cash. As we were leaving the bank with the money that we needed to travel to America, a man hanging around outside the bank grabbed it right out of my mom's hands. It happened so quickly. One moment we had the money that we needed to move to the USA, but the next moment we had nothing! In only a few seconds our hopes, excitement, and dreams were all stripped away.

I still remember her tears of desperation as she sobbed outside that bank, leaning against the wall, but there was nothing I could do. I was only 9 years old when this happened and I had never experienced anything like this. All I could do was give my mom a hug. Mom was the strength of our family, she always was, and always remained so. She took a deep breath and we left for home, with nothing. She would never accept defeat and we decided we had no choice but to start again by gathering the money we needed to leave Mexico in whatever way we could.

We sold most of our household items and I did my part by creating a tostada stand (like a lemonade stand) to sell food and drinks to do all I could to help collect money to come to the USA. It was when we were selling all our belongings and we were seeing our home slowly becoming emptier and emptier, that I came to realize that this was it. We were moving and come what may our lives were about to change forever. As if things weren't tough enough for us making that money back that had been stolen, I got stung by a scorpion and almost died. I can tell you being stung by a scorpion hurts very bad!

My older brother and I also sold tacos and Mexican bread at the local events, for a few pesos each, to help out with collecting money to come to the USA. After a couple months of hard work, selling everything, and working hard to make the money back, we had finally collected enough money to leave Mexico.

My mother was well known in the local community and was an active member of the school parent group in Tecomán Colima. My mom would make tacos Tuxpeños (traditional tacos from our region) and take them to the school for the kids that didn't have money for school meals. This kept her very busy, and we seemed to know almost everyone in our community.

With my father's service as a police officer, we had just enough money to live on, and in fact, we were considered a low middle-class family. We were always a frugal family, and we were never able to buy the luxury things that others bought. This was another big reason why my mother wanted to leave Mexico but not just for the luxury goods. She wanted more opportunities for us.

We read in the newspapers and watched on TV that kids were getting kidnapped and were getting killed daily. This was becoming normal in parts of Mexico. But keep in mind, this was in certain regions and neighborhoods but it was not all over Mexico. I remember sitting in the plaza with our friends and hearing stories of the latest kids that had been kidnapped or killed. I was so scared. All over the community kidnappings were being talked about and there was fear all across Mexico.

My mom was determined for us to have a better future, a better education, and a better life. She saw as we did also, that if we stayed in Mexico, we would probably get married young and have a family instead of pursuing any career and improving our lives. Dad was the role model of what we could expect there and mom definitely did not want that for us. My siblings, our mother, and I were a close family and our mom was the reason. She was the rock and made sure we had everything we needed.

Mom made the decision that we would all leave Mexico for a new life in America and we knew that once we left there, our move would be permanent. All of us were prepared to leave our way of life; with the risks, we could now see reaching closer to home.

Many of our friends wished us well and were sad to see us leave, but some, including our close family members, were angry that we were leaving. I thought maybe it was that we would be missed, or maybe because they saw we were making a new life for ourselves. Part of me thought they might have been a little envious that we were prepared to move away rather than accept what we had. But the decision had been made and that was that!

One day while my parents were in the kitchen, I listened in on their conversation. I recall my dad telling mom that they were finding bodies and body parts cut with ice picks at a soft drink company. He also was telling her that they were finding tips of fingers in soft drinks. I heard this same story again as I walked with mom to the "Mercado" (market). I was so scared. Seeing the newspapers full of children who had been killed, which added to my anxiety. This had become a normal conversation in our community. It was very scary and traumatizing for me to hear and to understand that living in fear was my new reality.

My little sister went missing for just a few hours and we helped mom to look for her. She reappeared a few hours later. That was scary. Mom knew that we were lucky she had returned. The fear of kidnapping was always there in the back of our minds. She was not missing, but had ended up going to see a friend at 4 years old!

But children going missing is also happening in many other countries too, not just in Mexico. Little success has been achieved, over decades, to curb this terrible situation. From my experience, I felt unsafe and unprotected by simply being a kid. The kidnapping of kids was now trending in our community, too.

I will always have hope that things will change, but it will take the combined effort of ordinary people together with the government and the police acting as one to drive down the crime rate from the country. It is a dream most people want to happen. I have always felt dreams can lead to an opportunity that, when acted upon, can then lead to achievements.

At the time in my neighborhood, it was normal for women to marry young and to have children. A woman who worked or attended college was viewed as socially unacceptable at that time in my small city. For me, I had no idea what I wanted to do, but to have the opportunity to see what I could do was very important to me.

We are all responsible for our own path through life and we cannot blame anyone or anything if we do not achieve our own success, whatever that success will be.

I had high hopes that America will offer me new opportunities.

Chapter 2:

Living The Dream

It's ok to be an outcast. — Blanca Blanco

I was 9 years old when we finally left Mexico. The trip was long and arduous. We first arrived at my grandma's house in Watsonville, California. She took us in for a few months, which really helped us a lot. Grandma had always wanted her family close to her and now this was the first step. My aunt's (mom's sisters) were very supportive and sweet to us, not only that but they had earned an education and had become independent successful women so it was refreshing to see that. They definitely inspired me. Gracias Tias!

My mom was just like her mother. Nothing was impossible for her and no work was too hard. I loved her for that. She, together with my grandma, were my life's role models. My grandma was our rock, as was our mom, and she was our number one supporter. She encouraged the trip for us and gave my mom constant support and encouragement and now her own dream was to have us all closer to her and living in America, which had now come true.

We had decided to live up on the northwest coast in Washington State in beautiful Lake Chelan. Our father had heard that he could get a job there working in the apple orchards. After a few months, we left my grandma's house and my aunt drove us all to Lake Chelan in her Nissan. We made our way north eventually arriving in Washington State. Speaking no English, in the beginning, was very hard for us. We also had to find somewhere to live but we had a small amount of money we had saved and some that our grandma gave us, from her savings. This was just enough to get us through those difficult first few months until dad found work.

When we arrived we had nowhere to stay, but we eventually managed to find a place. What we found was a garage that the owners allowed us all to stay in provided we paid them rent. I should add here that the owners were my father's own family. This garage was all we could afford with the small amount of money we had saved. Dad found work in the apple orchards and we saw that his work was very hard indeed. Because we didn't have many other options, we had to live in that garage for almost 2 years with no hot water, no shower, and a small toilet that seldom worked.

My parents, myself, and four siblings (I'm keeping their names out of the book for privacy purposes), their birth order was, older brother followed by me, then my 2 sisters and little brother.

We couldn't shower in our garage because didn't have hot water. Anyway, it did not have a shower or tub hookup. They also removed the toilet at times when they had prospective buyers looking at their home. Sometimes they locked us all up in that garage, for hours, whenever they had people coming to view the house. They had decided to sell it (this small detail they didn't tell us).

Winters in Washington State were frigid and the water we brought into that garage, in buckets, was so cold we had blisters on our hands from washing our clothes and dishes in such freezing water. But at least we had a roof over our heads, and for that, I was grateful to my parents.

We had electricity that lit two bulbs that operated by pulling a string; one over the sink and one over the toilet. We had an outlet and now we could use a small electric heater. It didn't prevent ice from forming on the walls around us and sometimes the electricity would randomly quit working altogether. Even when we were freezing and the weather outside was sub-zero, we remained in the garage huddled around a small heater, that we were able to buy, trying to keep warm.

It wasn't until recently that my mom told me some of these details, as I had blanked them out of my mind. She also reminded me that when I went to school, during the winter months, I had blisters on my hands from washing the dishes in that frigid water.

We sometimes forget these things as a way of carrying on with our lives because remembering them can be hurtful to us. In writing this book, I want to use my experiences as a tool to help motivate all who read about my experiences. The good and not so good, you will see how I tried to achieve the things, how I could dream to achieve rather than allow negative or past bad events that occurred in my life to be an eternal limit. I want to also show that childhood poverty did not define me, and that was my biggest fear as a kid, to be just another statistic. It was this constant fear that drove me to never allow this to happen to me ever again.

While living in the garage was difficult, it was the only option we had at that time. My father's family rented us the garage, which kept us from being homeless. I will always be grateful to them for looking out for my family. That experience provided me with so much personal growth, skills, and resilience. I am only sharing about the hardship of living in that garage to encourage others that may be in a similar situation as I was, to know there is hope and you can break that cycle. You can move forward no matter what your prior difficult experiences are.

My parents could not speak any English and our father could only work at laboring in the local Washington apple orchards earning just $4 per hour. That was it! $4 per hour to feed a family of six (my little brother wasn't born yet)! To say this was a cultural and financial shock doesn't even come close to what it was like for us.

But my mother, myself, and my siblings were a close-knit family. We trusted the decision to come to the USA. We believed that it would be far better for us in the long run.

Dad's earnings as a laborer working in the orchards was a big drop from what he earned as a police officer in Mexico, which was no more than a low to average weekly wage there. He earned just enough, not more than that, and certainly not enough for the inherent risks he took every day as a cop. But also, the fear of getting kidnapped was not with us now, so we had a sense of comfort in knowing that.

Now that we were living in Washington State, mom took on a job as a full-time babysitter while we were at school. She did this work for the 2-years we lived in that small garage and the following years in the trailers. I leave this part to your imagination. Yes, it was that hard for us all. We had to shower at a neighbor's home and sometimes some of our kind relatives let us use their shower.

We had to use a bucket literally for everything. There was a bucket for water to cook with on our single hotplate. We had to fill the buckets with water each and every day, one bucketful at a time.

Some of the kind people that we got to know around us, gave us blankets and clothes to keep us warm in the cold winters of Washington State, where believe me, it was bitterly cold in winter. I know it is difficult to imagine anyone living for 2 years inside a garage, a family of six, soon to be seven! We had no beds only the hard floor and a broken couch with my sisters and me doubling up to keep warm at night. But we had no choice and we all knew we had to make it work. I often went to sleep wearing 2 coats and 3 pairs of gloves. I could see my breath from the cold temperature inside that garage. During winter, the Chelan Elementary school secretary Jean would see us without gloves. Over the years, she began giving me and my siblings many pairs of gloves and coats. She would tell us to let her know when we needed more. I will always remember her kindness and determination to help us.

I could see that this was breaking my mom's heart, but nothing would stop her now. Here we all were, having to make do with very little and with my dad working in the orchards and mom working so hard as a babysitter being paid $5 per day for each baby! She looked after them for 12 hours each day for just $5 per day only taking on up to 5 kids and earning $25 per day.

The kids she was babysitting were the kids of the orchard workers, and for many, it was the only way they could work. They trusted my mother to look after their kids and it was not so much the low pay; it was more to do with the fact that they could only afford to pay her this, as they too were working for as little as $4 per hour.

My dad took on any odd job he could to earn extra money to help us make ends meet. He often came home with his sore hands covered in blisters and aching all over. But he never complained and nor did my mother.

Deciding To Make a Change

Winters in Washington State are bitterly cold and often we had ice on the walls inside the garage because of the sub-zero temperatures outside and inside. It was so cold it froze the water we had in our bucket. We huddled up to keep warm, and it was during those nights that I made a promise to myself.

What I promised was more than just a simple, "I promise," it was an oath. My oath to myself was that this would be the only time in my entire life that I would have to live like this. I would do whatever it took to *break the mold* and in doing so, I would make my life a success.

My promise became the driving force that gave me the passion to want to succeed in whatever I chose to do. But I was 9 years old at that time and no matter what I chose to do, I was determined to succeed. Nothing and no one would ever stop me from succeeding and I was certain of this.

One of the things I did was that at age 9, I organized and produced scenes with my sisters and we acted in our homemade plays. It was also a way to escape our current life and be in someone else's life, by creating characters and using our imagination. Acting gave me a sense of strength, as all the broken emotional pieces would come together in our plays and make me feel happier and alive.

During those early months, when I went to school, because I didn't speak, nor understand any English at all, it was a challenge and very embarrassing. I could hear people saying things I couldn't understand and I could see people laughing and talking but I could not understand a word they were saying.

At school, the standard English lessons were for students who could already speak and understand English. Our first months at school were very difficult for us. The school did have extra-curricular English lessons for us, so learning English was a slow process.

At night, when each of us got home from school, we worked together to help each other to learn English; although it helped, it was still a slow process. Can you imagine learning math, geography, looking at maps, but not understanding anything of what was written, said, or explained.

In hindsight, although the school turned out to be good for me and I excelled, it was mainly because of the promise I made to myself and my determination helped me to work harder. I have to be very honest, these early times trying to live the dream were the hardest times of my life. We had to do the best we could because we were all in this together, and failing was never an option.

Every night I dreamed of my future and how hard I would work to make it happen no matter what work I had to do, or where I would live, I knew would make it. I prayed almost every night and sometimes I cried quietly to myself in those frigid winter nights, forcing myself to think only of making my dreams of success come true.

I knew that I had to take action to reach my goals. Also, I knew it would be hard work. I began visualizing my goals for the future, I just needed to learn how to navigate through changing the negatives to positives. The key was to remain consistent during the process, which was very challenging.

I learned later that what I was doing was "re-framing" or shifting my thoughts to happy things, which was a healthy way of dealing with these difficult times. My frame of reference was not very wide, up to then, because I had so few happy moments, except when our mom would start singing a Leo Dan song and we would join in. That always made the mood lighter. She always loved his "música romántica."

Chapter 3:

My Early Days at School

A promise made is a promise to be kept. — Blanca Blanco

When I started school, I didn't want any of my classmates to know my living conditions because I knew it would separate me from them as "that poor kid." I didn't want people to see me or treat me differently and also, I was somewhat ashamed. I desperately wanted to just be viewed as a "normal" kid.

But my first days at elementary school were weird. I was treated like an alien with classmates looking strangely at me, asking me where I came from with an accent like that! I told them I was born here, although it was hard to believe, and they laughed in my face. They would make fun of my name over and over; like why I have the same name twice, it would hurt my feelings dealing with that all the time. I would tell myself, someday my name will be famous and you will regret teasing me.

Quite often when I was traveling to school on the bus, I found I was crying to myself, while looking out of the window so no one would see. I was so sad at how hard our life was for me and my family,

33

especially for our mom. But I kept this to myself as I never wanted anyone to know about my private life or my feelings. It was for me and my family to deal with, and it had nothing to do with anyone else.

I can also say that, later from my training in psychology, wanting to be seen and treated as an ordinary school kid was perfectly normal. I wanted to be seen as the same as any other kid at school. This is what most, if not all, children in my situation living in conditions like mine, or in children's homes, foster homes, or orphanages want as well. They just want to be seen and treated as no different from all the other kids. I certainly didn't need sympathy and I was just fine.

Though I was learning English as fast as I could, it took time and much of my early school life was in silence not being able to speak English and not being able to understand it either.

During those dark times, for my family and me, I had made my own life-altering decision, like the one my parents had made to start a new life. I was going to make sure I would be successful no matter what it took for me to reach my goal, no matter how hard it might be. I didn't know how, but I knew for certain that I would make it happen.

This was the beginning of my drive to succeed and do whatever it took to ensure I made it possible to achieve my goal of breaking through the invisible barrier that prevents us all from achieving our success. Mine had been created by the poverty my family and I were living in and this would never do for me. But as I later learned, it is not up to others to do this, it is up to ourselves to make our lives all that life can be. Certainly, I needed help, which was readily given but we are the driving force in our lives, no one else is. A promise made would be a promise kept!

Chapter 4:

A Trailer Park Kid!

Move forward; it's even harder to go backward. — Blanca Blanco

After just over two years, we found a tiny trailer to live in, and though it was a single trailer, probably built for just one or two people we were now a family of seven with one tiny room and a bathroom as big as an airplane restroom. It was smaller than our garage and not nearly big enough for a family of seven, but to us, it was luxury compared to our "garage home." After all, luxury is relative, isn't it? What is luxury to one person is not to another.

Our trailer was in a small trailer park, with a few other trailers, so I was now a "trailer park kid." I thought to myself, "Someone up there has a sense of humor!" But things were slowly improving and at least we weren't living in that rat-infested garage. We placed plastic on the door and windows, which did little to keep the cold out. Our sleeping arrangements for my two sisters and I were that we shared the couch, top to tail, which we swapped every other night. It was the only way we could all manage in that trailer. But whereas the garage had rats, the trailer did not, it only had mice. Oh, wait! The trailer had cockroaches too, and in the summer, the snakes slithered in and joined us.

We make our own way in this world and for me, at 9 years old these were the parts of my background that made me who I am now and I'm telling you how it was for my family and myself as a reference point to who I became later. At that time and ever since my biggest fear has been that I would remain in poverty, but that became the driving force for me to succeed.

As we were slowly digging our way out of our situation and after living in that tiny trailer, we eventually managed to get into a bigger trailer, and it was close by. In that trailer park, there were only 3 trailers. So, by trailer park standards, we were now trailer park snobs in our larger, two-bedroom trailer! Though this, of course, was not true at least we were moving up, half a step at a time.

The park was owned by a retired cop who was very nice, but there was a problem with the water system he provided. There were dead rats that we found in the water tank. Not only were they dead, but they were also bloodied as well! So how did they get there? My siblings and I were constantly at the doctors for random sicknesses.

At one point while we were living there, some of the people living in our trailer park got sick because the water supply to the trailer park was so bad. The water system was not working properly most of the time, especially in the summer, and we were only able to get water from a tank that was filled and brought to us from the cop's house when he remembered to fill it. When it was filled, we could all get water to shower, drink, wash our clothes, flush the toilet, and do other things that most take for granted. At this point, I can say that using the school bathroom helped me a lot and I made sure that I used those facilities every day as that was luxury compared to our trailer.

This means on the 1st of the month the water tank would arrive. This was to supply 3 families. Once the water tank became empty and the water ran out, we could not wash, shower, or have anything to drink until the tank was refilled. It was this water that made many people living there sick. By the 6th of the month, the tank was always empty.

We lived there in that second trailer from when I started middle school until I graduated from high school 7 years later. When my brother and I eventually left for college, my family had more room in their two-bedroom trailer! My dad stayed at his job until he retired and although he managed to get small raises, from time to time, he stuck with it and was faithful to his boss. At least I admired this about him.

Our Dad

Even though we had been struggling financially, my dad found a way to spend money on cigarettes and alcohol, which caused constant stress between him and mom. We could see how much she suffered from that, as we all did. He was a heavy smoker and smoked two packs a day. Only after he was told by the doctor about how dangerous second-hand smoke was for a newborn baby as well as for us children and with constant reminders from our mom, he finally gave up cigarettes. But he did not give up alcohol.

As a teenager, until recently, my father would constantly insult me by saying that I was "seca" which refers to outer attributes such as an unattractive skinny, gaunt, or scrawny girl. As a child, I was very insecure about my self-image, because he would call me a disgusting flat skinny person and would constantly say who is going to want "that" body. As I grew older, I began to embrace who I am and self-created a positive image from within.

Chapter 5:

Prejudice and Racism

I have a dream that my four little children will one day live in a nation where they will not be judged by the color of their skin but by the content of their character. — Martin Luther King Jr.

I was reluctant to include this chapter and to use the derogatory terms referred to here, but they were said and directed at me and my sister. I apologize in advance if these terms offend anyone. I want to be transparent about my life and since my family and I had experienced prejudice firsthand, I decided to include our experiences.

Prejudice and racism are often experienced by immigrants throughout the United States and all over the world, which I experienced often. I remember on one occasion when a school teacher was organizing a soccer group for physical education and he said, "To make it easier, let's divide the groups. The beaners on the right, and rest on the left side." I was very offended and hurt by his words and I asked my friends to go with me to report him to the office.

However, as we got close to the office, everyone left my side because they were afraid of being suspended for not being in class and perhaps the office, at that time, wouldn't believe us. So I also had to turn around and head back to the PE class. I experienced hopelessness because I felt in my heart that it was wrong to be treated that way. Being called a "beaner" after the effort I had put into my work was degrading to me and I became aware that some people in authority saw me as unequal to them.

On another occasion, my sister had told me her teacher had also called her a "beaner" and I shared with her that it was not appropriate language and I told her I would go to the school and report the incident. We reported it together, and after that day that teacher did not call her a beaner anymore. But the damage was done and regardless of her not using that derogatory term, we knew what she was thinking and how she and possibly others saw us.

It is important to remember to be kind especially if you are in a position of influence over others. It is important also not to assume all immigrants are here illegally because, in my case, I was born in the USA. Often I would hear the words "go back to your country."

On another occasion, while I was still in high school and working at the grocery store deli, a customer refused my help and requested an "American" person to help him instead. It hurt my feelings, but I had to accept his request and I moved over to help other customers.

Even in Los Angeles when I worked as a social worker for hospice patients, sometimes I would get removed from cases I was appointed to work on because families or patients wouldn't want people of color working with them.

I was often called a "wetback" even though I was born in the USA. It was such a derogatory term but was a common slang word used often to offend immigrants.

But I worked hard daily and I did not allow this negative belief to affect me, instead, I took action. I worked on educating people around me about treating people with equality and respect. We all have the same organs under our skin that define us as humans. So how illogical it is to treat a person differently when, based on science and anatomy, we are the same. Being a survivor and thriving despite experiencing discrimination, at all levels, takes so much courage for us Latinos and others to deal with. This challenge makes us stronger, not weaker.

I wanted to include the prejudice I experienced as it was there in my background. Despite all my hard work throughout all my schooling and in my later work with hospice care, it left its mark on me and my family. It is in my nature, to remain focused on what needs to be done and continue on my path to *break the mold*. I, like many others, pushed this prejudice behind me and tried not to allow it to affect who I am.

Living in poverty also is a major contributor to being discriminated against. As an example, on March 25th, 1998, I wrote in my journal, that I shared with one of my dad's family members that I wanted to attend college, she replied "I feel sorry for you guys, your future is only in this town. You guys cannot afford food, how do you expect to go to college. You are all going to be losers."

It hurt my feelings deeply because I knew the situation that we were living in and perhaps she was right. However, after a few weeks of feeling sad about her statement, I told myself, I don't want to be a statistic. Instead, I want to be a NEW statistical number that thrives with those in this category living in poverty. I have big dreams to attend college, earn an education, and be a successful actress.

I took a positive stand on that conversation; I was not a victim instead I was a survivor. No matter how someone contributes to our situations, one cannot blame others for making us feel bad. The only person solely responsible for how we act and feel is YOU. I decided to change the negative of her statement to positive self-talk to understand my thought pattern and challenge it. To change my life trajectory, I needed to take action and you will see throughout my book the tools and techniques I share to accomplish it.

Chapter 6:

High School Days

We achieve to the extent of what we invest. — Blanca Blanco

Lake Chelan, where we lived, was just on the edge of the Okanogan Wenatchee National Forest. I attended the local Lake Chelan middle and high school, in Washington State, from primary school all the way through to college. School, for me, was a slice of heaven. I threw myself into my schoolwork because of my thirst for learning. I found reasons to stay in the building as long as I could. It was warm in winter and cool in summer (more luxury than at home).

I knew if I ever wanted to go to college, which was part of my dream, I could only do it only by earning a scholarship since there was no possible way we could afford to pay for it. I became a nerd but I didn't care. I would work as hard as I could to get to college. My goal in life would be reached one step at a time but I would nevertheless get to where I wanted to be. I was a tomboy in school, a jeans and t-shirt girl. I didn't wear make-up or high heels until I was in Los Angeles years later.

Christmas was a difficult time for us because at school, after each Christmas holiday we were supposed to tell the class what we all got for Christmas. In my case, it was a new pair of socks or an item of

43

clothing, or a puzzle missing a few pieces, that we got from the Salvation Army. I dreaded that time in the year and did not want to tell them anything at all. But for me, these were great gifts.

As I saw it and from what I knew from my personal experience, it was, after all, not what I got but who the gift came from. The value of that gift to those, like me, who received it no matter how small it may seem to others, was a treasure to me. Although my parents did not have the money to give us gifts, they spent hours waiting in line, at the Salvation Army, to get us a gift. That meant so much to me especially when it was freezing cold outside, snowing, or raining outside. They walked home carrying bags of presents to make it a special Christmas for us, and they did, make a special Christmas for us.

For me, this was the true meaning of giving and receiving gifts at Christmas. Since my siblings and I had no money, we used to make presents and draw our own cards to give to our parents. Mom loved that even more as we had thought about what to give and had spent time creating each present. I loved making sugar-free, fat-free cheesecake for my mom and family during the holidays. Those days were always filled with magic for us all.

Anyway, life at my school settled down and I loved working hard at every assignment I was given. I joined the sports program and started to do track and field, and volleyball. What I liked most was that being at school and staying late, to participate in sports, meant I didn't need to spend more time in our tiny trailer.

Living in the trailer really was one big reason I did so well at school! Who would have thought that being a trailer park kid would be my motivation to succeed?

People have since asked me, "What did you do in your spare time?" This always made me smile, as I did not have any spare time at all. But to entertain ourselves, my siblings and I would learn songs and makeup plays acting in them in our tiny trailer. I loved doing this, it seemed to trigger something that I really couldn't explain. Maybe I was being given a sign of things to come!

Acting even as a young girl, took me to an imaginary place and I could become whoever or whatever I wanted to be. All I had to do was imagine who that person was, then write it and for a few short minutes, I was who I imagined myself to be.

I enjoyed doing this so much that I had to put it in the back of my mind when I was at school. Nothing, not even my love of acting, would come between me and my education. I also saw we didn't have many opportunities because I witnessed and saw for myself the hardship that existed for anyone without an education.

My school was quite small and was for me a great place to learn and do well. Because of this, if someone intended to do well, they could, and I did do well at that school.

My dad hated that I was traveling for sports meetings, playing volleyball, and other track events. He would say, *This is not right for a Latina girl, to do sports. Sports are for boys!*

He wanted me to get straight home after school and not stay late doing these activities. I couldn't understand why I was not allowed to be on the school track team, even when my brother was there with me and he was the star runner on our team. The first few weeks when I came home after my training, I was so sore and in pain from all my training. I walked into our home and he was so enraged holding his belt and ready to hit me or punch me. He hit me a few times, but other times I would run away from him. That made him even madder. I wanted to fit in with my ideals, not with his ideals.

My mom supported me, especially when my dad was behaving inappropriately. His anger continued and he would hit me often because I refused to accept his rules about this. One time I told him that if he hit me again, I would call the police. We were now in America, not in Mexico so what had been our life there would, for me, not be my life here. Like I said before, in Mexico we couldn't call the police because he ran the station but we certainly could here.

Looking back, being a track and field runner helped me emotionally, it helped me deal with my traumas and helped with the healing. Running is very therapeutic. It feels like hitting a giant reset button and it makes me feel limitless. I also enjoy the endorphin rush of accomplishment after a race.

I never went to any of the school dances until my final year. I was crowned as one of the Homecoming Princesses. I took my sister with me as my chaperone. Luckily because of my sister chaperoning me, this time, I could go. Dad never wanted to give us any freedoms. I did not do drugs, nor alcohol, so there was no reason, for my dad, not to trust my judgment. It was a control issue for him — *machismo*.

I was bullied in my early days at school because my English was not very good, but I had nice friends and they were always supportive and we stuck together. Despite the bullying, I remained focused on my schoolwork. I learned that when bullies get no reaction and are ignored, they go on and find another victim. Not only was I dealing with bullies at school but also at home from my dad. But I gave as good as I got because dealing with my dad gave me strength and I refused to be intimidated.

Karma!

Some of dad's family belittled us because we were poor, but when I had become successful, they only reached out to me when they needed money and I refused to give in to their manipulation. I also learned, many years later, from my old school friends that those few who were always bullying me never moved away from that town. They remained local in that small community and didn't achieve all that they could have. Nature has a way of equalizing all actions into reactions. For those who thought they were so big at school, bullying others like me, they were not able to rise to their fullest potential.

My First Jobs

When I was 13, on my summer school breaks, I worked full-time at a local hotel as a housekeeper. I loved it, it was a way of being independent and away from home or more precisely, away from our dad. The first thing I would buy from my paycheck was groceries for my family. I saved my money and had enough money to buy my sisters an ice cream treat, which made us all happy. We were all laughing with ice cream all over our mouths. Even as I am writing this, I'm smiling at the memory, how cool is that! It made me so happy to give them such a little treat, and it meant a lot to them. We never had the money to go out for ice cream before. My sisters loved the treat, and we were all singing Celine Dion's song "My Heart Will Go On," in the car, eating our ice cream. It was a perfect moment for us all.

When I was 14, I turned in my application to work part-time at a Safeway grocery store. I checked the application every week with the store. The store manager, Tom, was nice to me and told me they were not allowed to hire 14-year-old's but as soon as I turned 15 he told me I could work there. Throughout the year, I would keep checking, and finally, I turned 15. True to his word, I was hired.

I was now able to work part-time as a courtesy clerk throughout the year. I loved the independence this job gave me. I gave some of the money I earned to our mom and I was able to help my family financially. My mom and dad didn't pressure me to work. It was a choice I made, and also working provided me the freedom I needed to feel independent.

At the grocery store, I was making $4.50 an hour, which was more than my father earned as a labor worker! I still remember the first paycheck I bought groceries and my first bikini that cost me 80 bucks! I still have that bikini and I was so proud of myself. Becoming independent while at the same time being a responsible student. I knew this job was a step toward my bigger goals. I also learned that without an education I would be working in jobs like this where I would not be challenged every day, for minimum wage. But that experience gave me the knowledge I needed to grow as a person.

Later, when I could drive, in my senior year at school, I got a fantastic job working for the U.S. Forest Service. They gave me a very cool green car to drive and I was a receptionist in their office. I worked there in the summer only but the pay, as well as the use of the car, was incredible and I could hardly believe it!

When I was 16 years old, I earned a scholarship and I was sent to Washington DC, representing both my high school and the state of Washington. It was a big highlight for me at that time. I went to the White House, visited the Capitol building, and other important places around Washington, DC. I met many other Latino students who were in situations similar to mine, and they too were doing well despite their humble beginnings.

This was a big motivator for me to do as well as I could to be successful like them. Little did I know at that time, I already was just like them. But perception is reality, and for me, at 16-years old I didn't see this. I needed to think like that to keep my self-awareness and to keep the pressure on myself to succeed.

There were only 2 Latinos per state at this conference. Although I saw those other Latinos doing well, it was rare for me to see very many Latinos in my area going to college.

Shakespeare said, "We know what we are, but know not what we may be." What that meant for me was that if others had made it to college, then so would I.

Some people might think that I missed out on my childhood, well in fact maybe by some standards I did. But for me, I just had to make sure I never lived like this again so everything I did at school was to help me achieve this. The personal growth I gained from that experience not only has prepared me but also provided motivation to excel.

My Guardian Angel

Everyone needs a guardian angel and mine was Mrs. Taylor, who was the school nurse and also a teacher. She saw something in me that was worth helping along. She went out of her way to help me all through from middle school to high school and even helped me to apply for the scholarships that I would need to get into college.

It was her encouragement to apply for scholarships I needed. My parents could not help me with this since they had not attended college and had no experience with scholarships. She guided me all through my school years and if not for her help and support, I am not sure that could ever have been able to afford college. We certainly didn't have the means or the financial capability to obtain any loans for college.

I feel I owe her so much and I now believe she was definitely my guardian angel. She counseled me and constantly motivated me to keep doing well. I am certain that she knew I could get through college with her help, and that would allow me to do far better than many who had more than I ever had and did less with what they had.

Mrs. Taylor came to our trailer sometimes bringing clothing and food for my family, so she knew our background. As for me, as I said earlier, I never told anyone where I lived or anything about my background because I didn't want them to give me that sad, "poor thing" look, feeling sorry for me, or for them to treat me any differently to all the others. I was just fine and I never looked to compare myself with others at the time. I only thought about where I was headed. Mrs. Taylor knew my background and never said anything about my living conditions to other students there at school. She never knew that my father was abusive. I was too ashamed.

Sometimes it is only through looking back at all we have gone through, all we experienced, and where we are now that we can see people in our lives who stood taller than others. Those are the people who improve the lives of others through their selfless actions, with loving help, given freely.

Mrs. Taylor is that person who I will never forget and to who, along with my mother, I owe a great debt of gratitude. So I can say it here for all to read, thank you, Mrs. Taylor, a school nurse and teacher in a small-town school who showed me how much I could do, and what I could achieve. I can never repay all your love, kindness and support, except to put these words of thanks to you here in my story.

Messages of Hope

After I left school, I got a message from another teacher, at Chelan High School, who asked if I could come to the school to show other kids who were not doing so well, how I had managed to become successful by not allowing my home conditions and being poor to prevent me from succeeding. I have to say here that it was because of their help as teachers, mentors, and life coaches giving me so much encouragement that I was able to succeed at college as an honor student with 3.8 to 4.0-grade point averages. I was on my way!

These were the messages I received from one of the Chelan High School teachers:

so I was having coffee yesterday with a lady and telling her about all the kids I work with who do give up and live in Chelan Falls, Apple Acres, are failing out of school, girls who have the same problems as you and she had read that article about you and brought it up. She said "we should get her here to talk to the kids!"

anybody can say try hard, get an education, don't be a statistic. But you have lived it and if you showed pictures of yourself, your family, your house....and it looked just like theirs.... well that would be powerful!!! 🙂

You could use your fame & influence to change lives!!

I was happy to send a positive message and I have done this for others who may be in the same situation that I was in.

I made a 13-minute graduation video to be shared with the newly graduating students and I was so happy to hear that it was well-received. When my book is completed, I would like to go back and visit my school, to give back to those teachers and staff, and to help motivate these children, and graduates, who are the next leaders of our country, and possibly leaders in other places around the world. I always felt I could do more because I saw there was such a need.

We are all responsible for our own future and this is the strongest message I could send to any other students coming from a similar background as mine, or even if they don't, the message is the same.

Each of us must make our own success, as we each perceive it to be. If my success can motivate them to achieve theirs, then that makes me very happy. In my motivational video, I let them know they should not allow their circumstances to dictate their future. I wanted to pass on my message that they can achieve all they wish if they have the motivation to do so.

A Message From My Teacher

Mrs. Vickie Taylor my mentor at Chelan High School, was asked about my time at school and her impressions of me, she had this to say:

When I think of Blanca, the term that comes to mind is 'perseverance'. Blanca's goal was to achieve a better life for herself by graduating from college someday. On a daily basis, Blanca took steps toward her goal. She took advantage of every opportunity presented to her and would not allow obstacles such as language or financial barriers to get in her way. When Blanca was a senior, she spent almost every day after school writing and often rewriting, school scholarship applications. Blanca was wonderful to work with because she worked so hard and was very appreciative of any assistance. At that time, I felt that Blanca's drive was remarkable and I was confident that she would achieve her dreams. It brings me joy today to see how successful Blanca has become. I am reminded of why I enjoy being a teacher in Washington State.

This meant so much to me, that someone I loved learning from, who took the time to help me when I needed it, and who I looked up to, thought so highly of me. I will treasure what she told me, in this message, all my life as a personal testament to my school days.

When I was growing up, I didn't think my experiences would help others. However, as I got older, I began to understand that there is a need for stories like mine to be told to help motivate others. This, for me, was a life lesson, in that we don't often know the truth of how others see us and it is a pleasant surprise to know we may have made a difference even to those who are there to teach us. But for me it was more than that, it was the beginning for me to give back, to return to others what I had learned through perseverance and hard work.

Our first trailer park home. I am holding our brother. We made the cake, shown here, with mom and my sisters and topped it with a koala and a turtle that we already had; part of our "trailer park" décor.

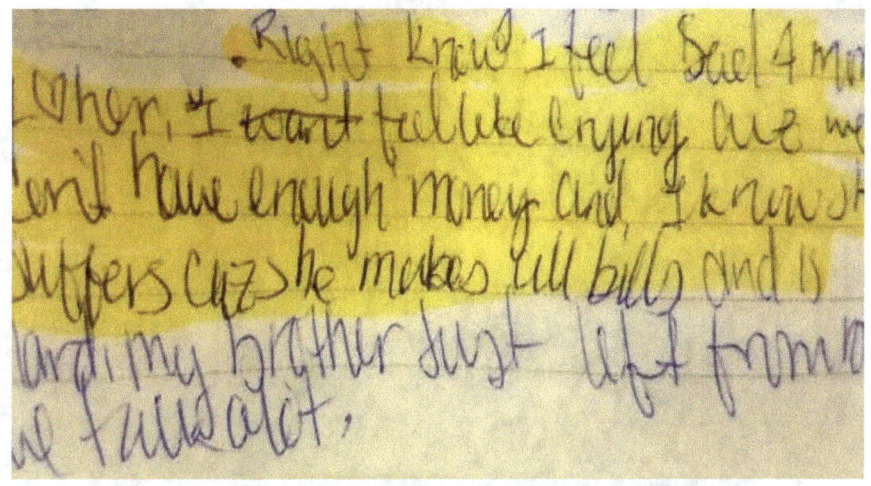

This is part of my journal, that I started writing at 9 years old. I wrote in English which was new to me when I wrote this, *".... Right now I feel sad 4 mom, I feel like crying and we can't have enough money and I know she suffers cuz she makes (pays) all bills and is hard. My brother just left the room and we talked a lot."*

My mom and me. I was always happiest next to her. She had
just bought me that dress. I treasure these photos.

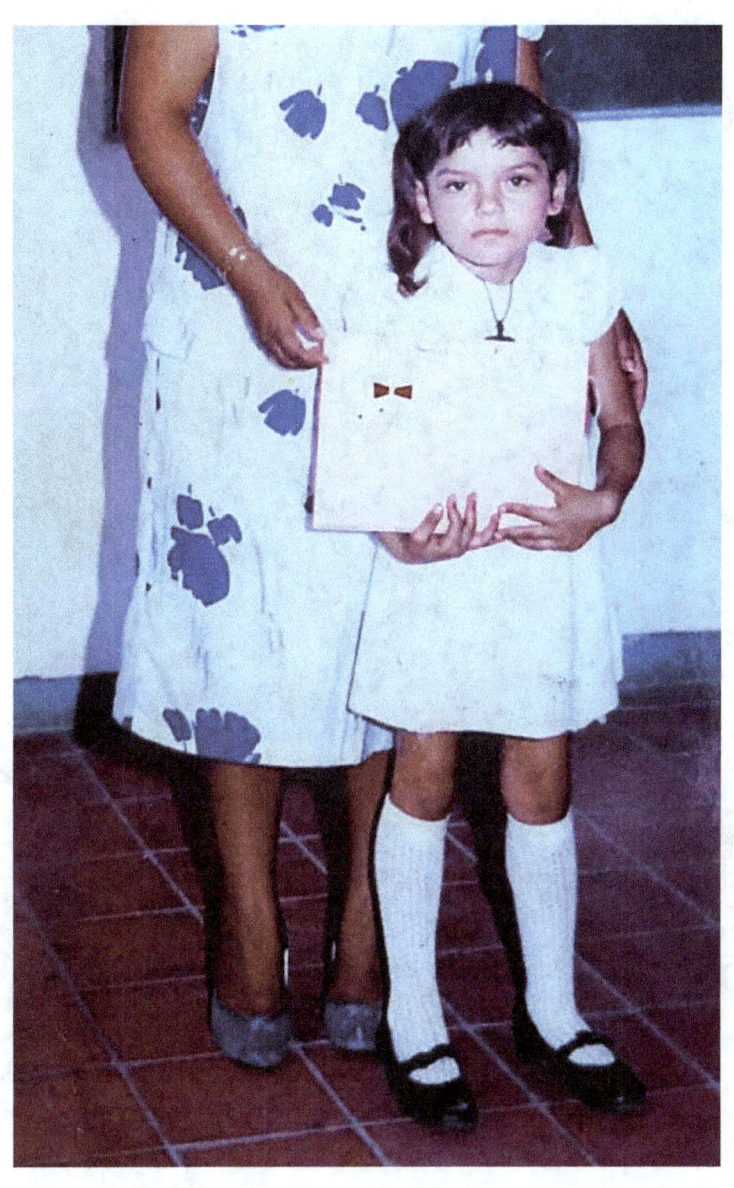

An early school photo taken in Mexico; I realize now how sad I looked in this photo. I was facing my father's abuse at this time...

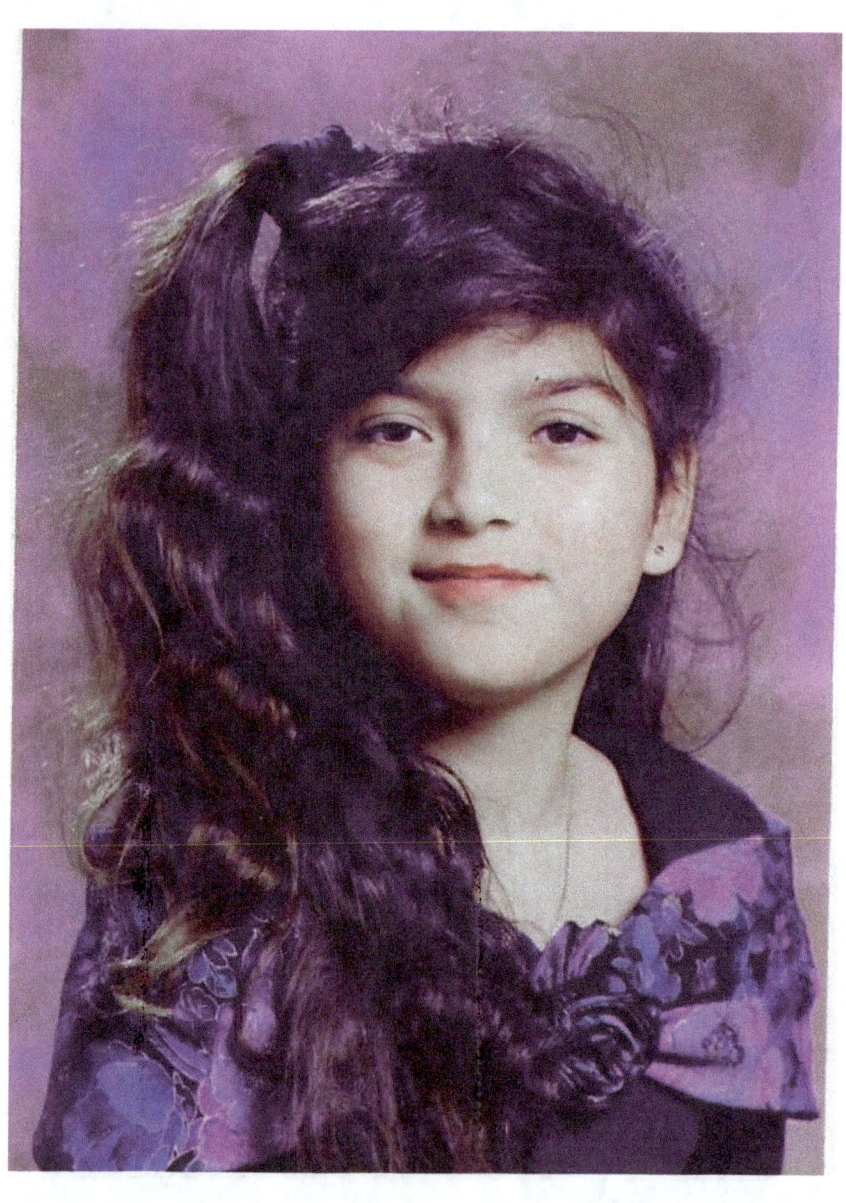

My first official school photo, I was 9 years old. My sweet grandma bought me this beautiful purple dress.

This is me posing. I guess I always knew I
would be in the fashion/entertainment industry.

Our second trailer park home, "luxury" compared to the garage we lived in before. My brother is in this photo.

My Track and Field photo. I loved competing in these events. They allowed me to be out from our trailer even though my dad punished me afterwards, but that didn't stop me!

Me inside our 2nd trailer home

Winters in Chelan were very cold and we couldn't afford winter weather clothing.

Me in my beautiful Quinceañera dress.

My undergraduate graduation photo from
Washington State University, (Pullman,
Washington). I was so proud of my achievement.

Chapter 7:

Undergraduate Degree

Education is not given it is earned, own it. — Blanca Blanco

I managed to get every scholarship I applied for because of Mrs. Taylor's guidance, so at last, I was finally leaving home to go to college. The college I attended was Spokane Falls Community College, in Spokane, Washington.

I had nowhere to stay and lived in my car until I eventually found 2 roommates. Sharing the apartment worked out well. We all got along great and they, like me, were hard-working and determined to get excellent grades. I also took on some part-time work. I was a Spanish teacher for first-grade kids before classes started. Then after classes, I was a hostess at a local restaurant and I also had a job as a caregiver at local homes for people with disabilities. Doing these three part-time jobs was enough for me to pay my rent and expenses, and enabled me to give my parents some money to help pay their rent. However, I quit the hostess job at the restaurant because I was corner by the manager in his office. He told me that he knew I needed a laptop that he would buy me one if I slept with him. I was shocked and disappointed, it led me to never go back.

My older brother also helped our parents out so now they were managing better than when we were living there with them. After my second year at college, my dad began to mellow a little, probably realizing that I was not only attending college but giving them money to help out. He eventually started to speak to me but didn't talk to me during my entire freshmen year in college, because he was so angry that I disobeyed him by wanting an education. In fact, on one occasion when visiting my mom and siblings, he refused to see the school newspaper I was showing him, where it mentioned me, making the honors lists with a 4.0-grade point average for the quarter. It hurt my feelings but also, I chose the path I wanted to take and was fulfilling my dreams so that helped me get through his anger. I fought him daily on these issues when I was in high school as I was constantly fighting for my independence and my own voice. I couldn't accept his gender inequalities and had to constantly fight for my freedom.

Anyway, for me, life was completely filled with my part-time jobs, my college work, and time spent in the library. I had to be disciplined with my time to fit everything in which suited my personality very well.

I was one of the first Latina's in our community to get into college so for me a goal had been reached and I was now famous in this small community (a big fish in a tiny pond). But strangely many of my Latino friends were not supportive of me going to college. They actually accused me of trying to be white! Can you believe that? I used to argue with them, "Exactly what is white about going to college?" They could never answer this except to try to convince me, just like my dad did, that it was not for us to be the same as the "white folk."

This illogical argument was ridiculous. Who lives our lives? Other people? Or, do we live our lives ourselves? For me, I knew I had one life to live and I would live it to the fullest and be all that I could be, despite the difficulties I had to deal with during my childhood. If those who tried to dissuade me from going to college wished to remain where they were, fine with me, but I will make my own choices, and going to college was one of them!

My time at college passed very quickly as I was constantly busy, but that is how I wanted it to be for myself. I saw keeping busy as a way of knowing I was moving forward towards my dream. Also, I was enjoying learning and improving myself every day and I was in constant hope of a better future. If any of us are to succeed, we must make our plans and stick to them.

Chapter 8:

Scholarships and Graduate School

You will face many defeats in life, but never let yourself be defeated.
— Maya Angelou

In order to meet the criteria and to be considered for the psychology program, I had to have a strong letter of intent, reference letters coupled with top grades, especially for Washington State University, which is an elite university and ranked in the top 10 in the country I also wanted a full ride so competition was high but I earned a full ride and was very proud of that. My grade point averages, being 4.0 certainly helped but as always with these things I had to prove I was worth the money Washington State University would invest in me and my further education.

For me to earn and complete my degree from Eastern Washington University, I needed to have a strong Competency Statement to graduate. The Competency Statement is summarized here. This is part of what I wrote and I hope you enjoy it.

Summary of my Competency Statement

As I continue to pursue my education, I realize the importance of a Master of Social Work degree. As a social worker, I will assist individuals, groups, and communities in need of advanced social functioning. My personal experiences triggered my desire to be a social worker for the betterment of others' lives advocating for the poor and social justice.

My practice philosophy includes an empowerment approach, diverse population-culturally competent practice, and respect for social work values and ethics.

Ecological Framework

Even though my family was poor, it led me to question at an early age, "who and what defines poverty?"

I had the opportunity to understand how people adapt to their environment and to find strengths within their traumatic situations.

Strength Perception

Recognizing and respecting people's strengths is fundamental for a social worker. If a client's goal is to attend college, we can work together to complete applications for financial aid to achieve the ultimate goal of attending college.

Empowerment

I have learned that when individuals make their own decisions, they tend to feel empowered by that control of their lives. In turn, they will open up more opportunities.

Diverse Populations

I am aware we are all different and I feel understanding behaviors and attitudes means being aware that we are all unique individuals and what may be typical for one may be atypical for another.

Social Work Values and Ethics

Research is an important component of what we do since it provides evidence of what could potentially work. I researched "attachment theory" and how parent-child influences brain development in the first three years of life.

My first degree was an Associate Arts (AA) degree from Spokane Falls Community College, before transferring to Washington State University for my Bachelor of Science degree in Psychology. I chose this because human behavior fascinated me. Personalities and human interaction were something I found interesting, learning what drives humans to take the actions they take. The principle of classical conditioning and operant behavior also fascinated me so much and was one of my favorite classes and training. I learned so much from the last student of BF Skinner, Dr. McSweeney at Washington State University.

Also, I had seen so much and I wanted to know why people did the things they did. I also wanted to learn how people could decide to change their circumstances and how to develop the motivation to do so. This was so important for me to understand exactly where we are and why.

I thought if I learned psychology I could understand and maybe help others. But as I learned more, I realized that some people just have no empathy. Another big reason for my choice was that I loved acting and had been involved in school plays whenever the opportunity arose. I thought a psychology degree would pair well with my love of acting and performing, as it would help to understand the psychology of my characters, the personality, behavior, action, and intentions.

My dad was still strongly against me going to college, university, or any higher education, telling me, *"College is not for girls like you."* He had the traditional machismo view that all young girls belonged at home, raising kids, cooking, cleaning, and doing nothing else. Well, the life he thought I should have was not for me.

I want to be clear on this, there is nothing wrong with wanting to be a housewife and a mother at a young age, but what we as women, want, is for this to be our decision alone, not a pre-made, or a foregone conclusion, or a decision made by a parent based on nothing other than what their life had turned out to be.

* * * * *

When I arrived in Spokane in my little car, I only had one blue basket of clothes, my big Winnie the Pooh bear, and 100 dollars from my savings. I spent about 8 hours a day in the library doing research for my classes. When I wasn't in the library, I was often in the cafeteria until it closed. Then I was up at the crack of dawn going back into the cafeteria so I was really not spending that much time in my little car. I had received scholarships but the funds were not given to me until I had attended the first week of school. I had arrived prior to starting, to prepare for my first day.

While I was in the cafeteria, I met a friend. We had met previously while we were doing our Track and Field meets in high school. She had an apartment and offered to let me use her couch, for $300 per month. It seemed like a lot but I had the use of a bathroom and other

74

things so, for me and from where I had come from it was well worth it. I'm certain that she will be a millionaire someday soon!

It was while I was in college when I met my first boyfriend. He and I worked together looking after people with disabilities at a private home. We only had time to meet once each week for coffee or lunch while we were in school because we were both very busy at the time. Despite this, we stayed together for 13 years (the equivalent of 3 Hollywood marriages!) But, as we both eventually realized towards the end of our journey, we each wanted different things from our lives together.

We had an amicable separation. As we got older, we saw our lives were running in parallel but we didn't see them intersecting. He wanted a low-key life settling in Washington State where we both lived and went to school but I wanted more than this. Though living in Washington State had its beauty, with mountains and a rugged coast, but I wanted to be an actress and I knew for certain the life that he wanted was not what I wanted and could not offer.

So after 13 years together, we parted ways. It was hard for me because he was my first love and only saw us growing old together. I realized, at that time, that love alone is not enough. There needed to be other elements to maintain a strong foundation in a relationship and having parallel goals leads to disaster, not to mention resentments, so it was hard but we had to take action and separate.

* * * * *

After I transferred into the psychology program at WSU, I did well with my degree and achieved a GPA of 3.9. I was very happy and proud of myself that I graduated with honors. Immediately after, I went on to receive my master's degree in social work and this, for me was the pinnacle of my education. They helped me understand human behavior and interaction. I also chose these degrees because they covered the family environment and how it affected people as individuals and in families. I had a good insight into this.

I was one of the first in my family to earn such a degree and had smashed right through the glass ceiling in doing so. My time at university for me flew by so fast! It seemed that one minute I was just starting my life there in college and the next I was leaving university.

Seven years had passed by and I was so busy with coursework and continuous studying that I never realized how fast time was moving for me but at the same time, I was enjoying every minute. It was such a good feeling to be learning every day, becoming an independent woman, and working towards accomplishing my goals without having anyone trying to destroy my drive. I figured if I am succeeding in academia, I can succeed at anything I set myself to do. I was also taking acting classes and workshops simultaneously but I was a strong believer that a foundation in academia was imperative.

I was also involved in the college clubs. One of them was the Latino Club where I became president; managing socials and club events, which I enjoyed being part of as these activities enabled me to meet many new people. My best friend was the secretary for one of the clubs. She became a successful scientist. We got along very well and accomplished a lot together.

What I loved the most about my college and university life was my independence to be able to go where I wanted and do what I wanted whenever I felt like it. I could do this because I was getting good grades and doing very well with my education. Learning for me was not difficult, in fact, it was enjoyable. My thirst for knowledge was always there and I could meet with my teachers and discuss any points I didn't understand. I always sat at the front for the lectures so I could see and hear everything. Plus, I wanted to make sure my professors saw me as a person, not a number. My freedom, from where I was at home, to where I was now, was a blessing!

It was hard work to earn the grades I received, and the results were all I could dream them to be. It was just a pet peeve of mine and so annoying when people would tell me "Oh you are so pretty. I bet it is not hard for you to get good grades," *really?* It felt like an insult. It *WAS* an insult! I never believe outer attributes have anything to do with intelligence. I know I am in a somewhat superficial industry now, but I strongly believe your looks do not help you get roles. It's your talent, hard work, and good work ethics that help to get you the roles.

Others at the university were there as much to party as to learn, but maybe they found the learning easier than I did. On Mondays and Tuesdays during lectures, you couldn't find many students present because they had been out partying all weekend. Then on Wednesday and Thursday, more showed up but Friday most were gone again to spend the weekend partying.

This partying life was not for me. I was more comfortable studying and getting good grades. I enjoyed the process of learning and that made it a fun and challenging task. Partying for me was eating Doritos in the library, studying 8 hours a day, with my friend Rosa.

Doing all-nighters for studying was also fun for me. Doing my research and going to the library as often as I could, *I loved it*. You could say that I was a "happy nerd"! I spent so much time on my studies, and it was for that reason, a lesser grade average for me, would be a failure. One doesn't work as hard as I did to have only average grade points.

I began to think about what I would do when I finally left university and one of my dreams was to leave Washington State and move to Los Angeles as I believed my future was there. I wanted to become an actress!

Chapter 9:

University Professors

The greatest sign of success for a teacher... is to be able to say, 'The children are now working as if I did not exist.' —
Maria Montessori

One of my teachers at Washington State University was Professor Ed Byrnes. Ed Byrnes is a professor of social work, teaching classes in Cognitive Behavioral Therapy (CBT) and Applied Behavior Analysis (ABA). His work resonated with me since as a child, I utilized some of his taught principles of "Cognitive Behavioral Therapy" on my own, but I didn't know I was doing that at the time.

Professor Byrnes was great to learn from and he was a gifted teacher who not only knew his subject extremely well, but he could teach it in ways that made learning from him a rewarding experience.

When I left University, I was told that Professor Byrnes, at Eastern Washington University (EWU), had been asked about me, this is what he wrote:

"Her journey is exactly the kind of narrative that motivates people to rise to their best capabilities," says Professor Ed Byrnes, who taught Blanco at EWU. "This may inspire people toward academic pursuits, yet I think her story encourages people to do their best in any avenue." Byrnes says the thing that struck him as remarkable about Blanco, as a student, was her intellectual versatility; she was as comfortable with science and quantification as she was with design and art. Additionally, says Byrnes, "When I consider the distance she has traveled in her life and the genuine humility with which she conducts herself, I believe that she is well-rounded in her heart as well as her intellect."

As a statement from someone I looked up to and admired, who saw me in my role as a student, to have written this about me was something I was surprised at seeing and happy to receive. How we see ourselves is not always how others see us.

I saw this as a confirmation of the promise to myself; to do all I could to achieve my goal of never remaining in poverty again. Professor Byrnes' comments reminded me of how hard work can lead to positivity.

We are not all wired the same and what for one person comes naturally, may for another be extremely difficult. But that is the beauty of who we are. We all have gifts we are given at birth and for some, those gifts are used in all they do. For others they may choose to do something else and not to use the talents they are blessed with, we all call this freedom of choice, or free will, which in itself is a divine gift.

I hope to show that hard work and a determination to do better for ourselves is something anyone can achieve. I managed this by creating small goals that collectively led to a much bigger and successful outcome.

Chapter 10:

My Internships

Condition yourself to turn thought into action. — Blanca Blanco

I did a lot of research on poverty and how severe poverty affects young people as they are growing up whether in poverty or in an environment, which placed children and families in a disadvantaged position. Research showed that if a person or family is experiencing poverty, then the chances are they will remain there. This is a sad fact of life and many organizations try to help stem the continuance of poverty but more and more people are homeless or unable to find work. The work they do find is very low paid and, in many cases, as I found through my research, does not get them out of poverty. Therefore, the cycle continues from generation to generation.

Many people become stuck and remain in poverty for their entire lives. I understood this very well as I too had been brought up in very poor conditions that many would have given up as a result. So for us, we had all chosen to better ourselves and to have a brighter future through education, college, university, and employment that we each were responsible to achieve. We sacrificed so much in the beginning when we moved to the USA, but in the long term, we knew it would pay off. Many teachers told me this and I can say as I got older I began to see it. When I moved out to go to college and looked at my life as an outsider I got to see how extremely poor we were. I knew we didn't have much but I never thought we were in severe poverty. Having a loving mom and siblings made us happy despite the poor conditions. Our richness came from within.

I learned there was another element in living in poverty and that was mental illness and other physical illnesses. When a person is diagnosed to have a mental disorder, they cannot afford to keep up with the high cost of medical treatment or more importantly the high cost of drugs all of which are incredibly expensive.

Once when I was working in Monaco on a film, I got very sick with a bad cold, high fever 104, bad cough, and was dizzy (this was before the Covid-19 pandemic) and the pharmacist recommended a doctor. So I went very early and I was stressed because I didn't have health insurance in that country. As I walked in, there was no receptionist, just the doctor's office. I told the doctor I didn't have insurance, he looked at me strangely and said, "That's not important to me. My focus is to treat you, let's do that first so we can get you a treatment." He assessed me first then wrote a prescription. His diagnosis only cost me $20 for his consultation. The prescription was just $10!

I wrote a paper on poverty, and the effects it has especially on children. I included it at the end of my book. It is a sad fact that poverty breeds more poverty but this trend can be broken through education and financial/social assistance.

The Going Home Initiative

For my master's degree in social work, I was required to undertake an internship. To meet these requirements, I selected the "Going Home Initiative Program." I would be working with clients who were in jail and I would be preparing them to reenter the community in hopes there would be a smooth transition. The program offered supervision and parole after release. The program ran from 2003 until 2007 and was funded by the U.S. Department of Justice through a $1.5 million grant and was started by President George Bush.

I was part of a team and we assisted case managers with developing an in-depth transition plan to guide the process for a smooth transition. I had never been inside such a facility where doors are locked after I entered and guards are always present. After they were released, we would continue to work with them from our office in Spokane. The teams were all there including supervision and parole teams.

I used my training to help prepare inmates, who were about to complete their sentence of incarceration. My supervisor was Percy who was excellent at his job and I learned so much from him.

I enjoyed this work as it gave me a purpose and some great and useful experience in using all that I had learned and been trained to do, but now I was applying this in real-life situations. The inmates had no idea how hard it would be for them to find a place, to find work, and to fit back into society or in a community that is inherently working against re-employment and rehabilitation for former inmates. My job was therefore to help them to prepare for what lay ahead. Our work in the community was very successful and received great support and recognition.

Working With New Young Mothers

I also went to Portland as part of my internship, as a Parent Educator. I worked with first-time parents, moms or dads, to guide them through parenting with their new child. My work was not so much how to do the daily feeds but more to go through their child's and brain development and show them ways to increase brain development, using words, music, and other tools to guide these new parents.

Better still, I got paid for my internship! I was the first in my class to get paid for this internship. So I got the necessary hours as well as the pay. I was not coming from a judgmental viewpoint but more from a learning perspective. But it also underlined my already formed view that being a young mother was not for me. I saw the hardships that being a young mother caused and felt that my strengths were in other areas.

While I was attending graduate school, doing my master's degree, I had acting workshops with amazing coaches. I had an agent and was doing auditions and felt blessed every time I landed films and commercials, and even small roles. Gordon Hunt would later say, "There is no small role, every element in the story plays an integral role." So my next life was already beginning for me.

One thing was for sure, I was never standing still, my spark and passion were always there. Despite my internships, which I enjoyed immensely, I knew all this was a foundation preparing me for the next stage of my life, to be an actress and to create different characters. It was like a deep-rooted burning desire for me and I knew I would do what it took to become an actress; training, learning the business, and going for as many auditions as I could.

Having made my decision to pursue being an actress, I left Washington State, on my way to my next career, in Los Angeles where I was going to become an actress. That was my plan! I said my fond farewells. I packed all my stuff and left Washington State and Portland, Oregon, which had been good to me, and made my way to Los Angeles, California.

Chapter 11:

Moving to L.A.

It may seem like forever, but doors do open eventually. — Blanca Blanco

While finishing my internship in Portland, I was taking acting classes, workshops and had an agent. In fact, I was getting booked in films, commercials, and music videos. I remember my first role in a music video was with the Everclear rock band who is originally from Portland. I was the lead actress. It was such a fun experience and Art Alexakis, the band's lead songwriter, vocalist, and guitarist was such a sweetheart to work with. It was a wonderful experience to be on set and it continued to give me that spark to continue with my dream of becoming an actress.

Between my paid internships and my acting, I was able to save money to become financially independent when I moved to L.A. I bought myself a BMW so I could move around for auditions and meetings with agents, producers, and anyone else I needed to meet.

I was now starting the next phase of my life to become an actress. I had no set schedule. I knew no one and I had to start from scratch. I found a job working as a social worker in hospice care, which was a very challenging job. But my work was to provide emotional support in hopes they reach acceptance for what they would be facing. I was paid well for my work, which added to my savings and would enable me to transition into my acting career with no financial issues.

My job, in hospice care, made me develop thick skin as I could not be seen crying or showing sadness or negative emotions on seeing these patients who were on their last journey. I had many job offers while I was in L.A. because of my psychology and social work degrees and the fact I was bilingual helped a lot. I have to say though, doing this kind of work changed me. The work made me focus on the moment as I realized none of us knows what lies around the corner in our lives.

The Lonely Rich

One thing I noticed with my work in hospice care was the big difference between the rich, the not-so-rich, and the poor families when it came to the final care of the patients. My caseload was as many as 40 cases at any one time and the people there came from all walks of life as we were located in L.A. One thinks of hospice care as being for the aged but this was not the case at all. Yes, the majority were elderly people but also there were young people in their 30s or 40s and even kids who for one reason or another had ended up in hospice care.

I saw many large Latino families that didn't have much in the way of property or income. When their family members came to us, a grandparent or parent, all the family members were there to help them pass. Their loved one was surrounded with comfort and love. Sometimes there wasn't even room for them all around the bed or in their room. But they all came anyway.

But our patients were made up of many different socioeconomic backgrounds. Some were rich and successful, even from within the entertainment industry, others were retired successful businessmen and business women, some people with accumulated or family wealth, were often in our care, but alone!

Few, if any, families of these wealthy people spent any time with their loved ones even knowing they were on their last journey. The family members of the wealthy, who did spend time with their loved ones, were often overheard asking them what would happen to all their money, who would get it? How very sad and what a statement as to the real success of these rich people.

For me this was a life lesson, in that, I knew I would make sure this would never happen to my family. I felt so sad for these people who perhaps had spent their lives being or becoming successful and were wealthy as a result, but now they were alone to face their passing with no one from their family to be with them. But one thing I do know is that they were often now alone facing their biggest challenge, which one day we will all face, death.

In a Disney cartoon based on the beautiful book, "A Christmas Carol", there was a scene where 2 goofy-like characters were digging the grave for Scrooge (who was a Scottish Donald Duck in the movie) and as they were digging one said, to the other, as he flicked his cigar ash into the grave they had dug, referring to Scrooge who had just died, *"Ay, He'll be the richest man in the graveyard."* How true these words were when they were said in a cartoon? Yet I was seeing this on a weekly, if not, daily basis.

I always saw myself, up to that point, as being grounded but this job "re-grounded" me. Seeing all that I saw there, the sadness the disappointment, and knowing the people there were all about to pass away. It made me appreciate living in the moment. Prior to this work I had planned all my next moves several moves ahead, like a chess game, and focused on making each decision happen in my future. But what I saw during my time working in hospice, changed how I saw my own life. I also knew that if I ever did reach success, I would still be in close contact with my family and friends.

Chapter 12:

My Acting Career Begins

Walk with confidence. YOU are a diamond. – Blanca Blanco

When I arrived in Los Angeles, I was not yet in the Screen Actors Guild (SAG). Even though I had gotten roles, they were not what was required to become a member of SAG.

I spent my time between acting jobs, continuing with my acting classes, and going to auditions. Of course, I still had my full-time job as a social worker.

On a side note, before I was working in the professional world working in SAG authorized movies, I worked in some pretty low-budget movies. The crew numbers were so small, that each person had multiple roles from sound, lighting, and stage management. Only a handful of crew members filled the roles of all the things a movie production required. It takes a lot of talent to be able to understand each department in movie production and I could see their strength and passion in bringing a story to life.

Auditions

Success in the entertainment industry does not happen overnight. It is a slow, arduous process. It involves many auditions, and afterward, hearing the word "no" more times than "yes." This is normal for anyone in the industry. Any auditions that resulted in a "no," served as a learning experience for me that I was able to apply to my next audition.

Kathy Griffin — The Groundlings

While I was at a dinner, sweet Kathy Griffin, highly recommended that I join The Groundlings. She said it was one of the best improv schools around. To join The Groundlings, one must audition. So I did. I prepared and following my successful auditions, I began taking classes there. It was great being silly and improv was so much fun. I still take refresher classes when I have the time between jobs. I have learned so much from this theater school.

I now had a new agent and manager, along with a strong portfolio and a reel. I was blessed to have been introduced to actor/ producer Charles Matthau (Walter Matthau's son). He provided guidance, important information, and also connected me with a couple of good agents. I will be always grateful for his support. The acting jobs I landed at that time were still non-union jobs. It was a *Catch 22* because I needed the work to be eligible to join the union, but the work was not union authorized.

Approximately 2 years later, I had enough professional work to finally join the Screen Actors Guild, which meant I could at last now work in bigger budget films or "mainstream movies." It also meant I could now work with more professional producers, casts, and directors.

I began studying acting under Gordon Hunt, Helen Hunt's father. This lasted for 10 years until he passed away. He had experience in not only training his daughter but also as a director. My training sessions were weekly and were extremely helpful in keeping me working on my craft. He was a great teacher. Working with a gifted coach felt amazing!

More acting roles were coming in for me, my work in hospice care could end, and I could now focus on my film/tv career. It was my passion and it was what ignited my soul. This was my dream and it was going to be my career, come what may!

One of my first major roles was in the 2008 feature film *Dark Reel* opposite Edward Furlong. I also had a role in a Lifetime movie playing a cop in, *Crimes of the Mind*. I watched it on TV and it also gave my family a chance to see me in my new career. They were so happy for me.

Gordon Hunt would tell us that when the audition is done, forget about it. If you land the role, great! But, if you don't, you've already moved on to the next opportunity.

So that's exactly what I did and it meant I didn't stress out after each audition. If I heard back great, a nice surprise, but if I didn't, well that was ok too and he told me, "Don't sweat it!". Although, I did prefer to get the parts than not to get them. Winning is always more fun than losing!

In the words of actor Albert Finney, who played "Uncle Henry" in the beautiful movie *A Good Year*, he tells his young nephew, a young Max, played by Freddie Highmore who, in the movie, just lost a game of tennis against his uncle, "A man learns nothing from winning. The act of losing, however, can elicit great wisdom. Not least of which is, how much more enjoyable it is to win. It's inevitable to lose now and again. The trick is not to make a habit of it." I had to smile at that line because that was me thinking about my many auditions!

There are so many variables that happen following auditions. The producers desire for one person over another, the casting director's opinions following all auditions, as to who is best suited for the role. This is vital to the success of any movie. Poor casting can ruin careers as well as a movie's box office success. Knowing and understanding this helped me to understand that losing is not personal. It will always be who is best suited for the part as a coordinated opinion.

My training in psychology helped in my progress as an actress. Not only to understand the roles I was auditioning for but also in dealing with the many losses I would have to endure, especially the roles I would have loved to have played. Make no mistake, we are turned down for more roles than we land. I don't want to preach to the choir, but this is important for any aspiring actor to understand, and is a reason why so many who have great potential, in movies, instead choose to follow other careers.

I knew also, from my workshops with Gordon Hunt, that being seen as desperate during auditions is a definite "no, no" and will undoubtedly lead to rejection. It will overshadow our ability to handle the audition exactly as the role demands. No one cares! Another thing here is that sometimes, following a successful casting, a writer, producer, or director may decide to change direction and re-cast for the new concept. These are all the components of the movie-making process and are never in our control.

We are trained actors so acting cool and not desperate should be a breeze! Even the most well-known and famous actors are sometimes not cast for reasons outside of their control, that's the movies!

Here's a funny story from a role I had in a commercial very early on in my career. I am quite tall for a Latina, not overly so, but on the taller side rather than the shorter. In one of the first commercials I was in, my Latino co-star was shorter than me, so they stood him on a crate when we were standing together in the shot. When the commercial came out, it looked like he was taller than me. I guess that's, *movie magic*!

Many well-known successful actors are quite short, but you would never know it. Movie magic strikes again! Obviously, height had nothing to do with their success.

It would be nice one day to audition and not to worry about the requirements like to be shorter than this, or be taller than this, olive or fair skin, straight hair, curly hair, be curvy, or just like the girl next door, not too pretty, rough-looking and just give people the opportunity to read and see what their soul brings to the character. Breaking the stereotypes can bring new layers to our thinking outside the box.

On a good note, at the time of this writing, I auditioned for a co-starring role in a movie. But after I got that part, the producer called me and told me that they were so impressed with my audition, they wanted to know if I would play the lead role! My answer was *YES!* I would love to play the lead! So all is not doom and gloom, we take the rough with the smooth.

Chapter 13:

Diversity In Movies

Diversity and inclusion, which are the real grounds for creativity, must remain at the center of what we do — Marco Bizzarri

A positive change I have seen for myself is that nowadays movies are more open to diversity. However, it is a very slow process and there is much room for improvement. We still need more lead roles for Latina women and equal pay, to name just a few. This has become apparent more so now than was ever the case before. Many successful actors and actresses, who are considered "minorities," are now playing great roles in the highly successful box office hits. They have paved the way for people like me.

While many Latina actresses have done amazing work and have achieved much success, two Latina women stand out in my mind as special to me, Rita Moreno and Salma Hayek. Without them, many roads would not have been paved. I have always idolized Rita Moreno and was so happy when we were cast in the film *Torch,* directed by Christopher Coppola. What an honor for me!

Rita Moreno is a force of nature! Because of her, there was a historical shift in the portrayal of all Latina actresses. I am going to share a bit of her incredible background.

Rita Moreno has been a force in the movie industry for 70 years. As an actor, dancer, and singer she has earned all four major entertainment awards; an Emmy, Grammy, Oscar, and Tony. There are only 16 actors, producers, directors, and composers who have been awarded all four.

She made her Broadway debut at age 13 and in 1950 made her first movie, *Young, So Bad*. After this, she signed with MGM and adopted the name, Rita Moreno. She was cast in ethnic minority roles to fill the studios' needs at the time. Even after winning the Academy Award in 1961 for her portrayal of Anita in *West Side Story*, the first Latina actress to do so, the studios continued to offer her roles that stereotyped ethnic minorities. Because of this mistreatment, she decided to leave Hollywood for almost a decade.

She returned in the 1970s and made several successful films, and was a main cast member in the children's series. "The Electric Company" on PBS for 6 years. It was at this time she won a Grammy for her contribution to the show's soundtrack. In 1975 she earned her Tony award for Best Featured Actress in "The Ritz" and in 1977 for her appearance on "The Muppet Show" she won a Primetime Emmy Award for Outstanding Individual Performance in a Variety or Music Program. This made her the third person in history and the first Latina to win all four major awards.[1]

Another one of my favorite actresses is Salma Hayek. I had the pleasure of meeting Salma at Creative Artists Agency (CAA). She was so kind and sincere when we met. I want to share a bit of her background. She has done some amazing things and has definitely contributed to paving the way and empowering women to break the mold!

---

[1] Womenshistory.org/education-resources/biographies/Rita-Moreno

Salma learned very quickly that Latina actresses were typecast and by 1992 had only received bit parts.

However, when Robert Rodriguez and Elizabeth Avellan gave Salma her first big break in the movie *Desperado,* from that point forward her career took off. She appeared in such movies as *From Dusk Till Dawn,* and *Fools Rush In,* which was her first co-starring role. By the way, I still have *Fools Rush In* in my personal movie collection.

I can remember watching Salma in *Frida*, loving every second of her brilliant performance. The movie was a box office hit, and I was happy to see it was nominated for 6 Academy Awards, including Best Actress, for Salma.[2]

Rita Moreno and Salma Hayek are still showing us that even though they have broken the mold for many there is still work to be done. Hint, hint, hint . . . *any producers reading this?*

Being an actor is highly competitive, there may be dozens who turn up for auditions all of whom may be perfect for the role. However, if you do your work, every day, our competition pool becomes smaller.

If we don't strive for success, in whatever that success may be, then we will never know if we could have made it and reached what we strived for. Sadly, there may be many things that work to prevent us from reaching our goals, but one thing is for certain, not having life goals will lead to a more unpredictable future.

I am someone who strives for success no matter what it takes. That is how I am wired and it is the same strength and determination God gave me to help me to cope with all I would face along the way. For me, setting my goals is part of that possible success.

---

[2] imbd.com/name/nm0000161/bio?ref_=nm_ov_bio_sm

Chapter 14:

Scams

If something doesn't feel right, most likely it isn't. Trust your intuition. — Blanca Blanco

I had a situation following a call for an audition as a TV show host. The show was something similar to *Entertainment Tonight* and I would be one of the hosts for the show. I met with the production company, auditioned, got callbacks, and all appeared to be legit. They offered me the job, and all seemed good. Then, they told me about the next step before starting. I would have to meet the executive producer, at a hotel, in his room and sleep with him! Naturally, I declined politely and told him that I would not be going to a hotel, nor would I sleep with the executive just to get the job and I mentioned how unprofessional that was.

He then told me if I didn't feel comfortable, they would have alcohol for me so I can relax and that it would all be confidential since the executive is happily married and have kids. *Really?* He just didn't get it! It all seemed so strange to me and so far away from my values and ethics.

No sooner had I declined, that they started to ridicule me saying I would never make it in Hollywood. I quickly left, now happy that I had decided on my gut reaction but also furious that they had threatened me in the way they did! The funniest thing was that he tried to normalize that behavior, by giving me a list of the A-listers that did this telling me how I don't understand the industry. I had to laugh at that!

On another occasion, I had booked on a project that was being filmed out of town. Upon arriving I was to check-in at the hotel and then they would pick me up to go to see the wardrobe department and sign contracts, it all sounded okay. The agent gave me the address telling me to meet the production team there. She gave me the name of the hotel and although I had a strong feeling about this booking, something about it felt uneasy to me. But I told myself to be careful and I asked a friend to come along. I had even asked a manager to check on this, to see if it was a legit offer and if a movie was actually being filmed.

They manipulated the situation and mentioned a few of the manager's clients, that they had booked for other work. She said, "Oh you are going to be okay we have worked together before." So, I thought okay, I will go and take a friend just in case. My intuition was strongly telling me something was not right.

I drove there with my close friend and when we arrived at the hotel, something just didn't seem right. Call it intuition, gut feeling, whatever, something didn't sit well with me. When we arrived, the person we were to meet was there and came out to meet me. He seemed professional as he was constantly on the phone, which was quite normal for a production crew member. I got my things while my friend waited in the car.

He told me we have to go onto the set, so I thought maybe this seems to be legit, and I went with him driving my own car to the set.

We were parked in the parking lot of a K-Mart. But as I walked toward him, I didn't see any trailers or people milling around as they usually are on a movie set. This made me nervous and I was now on alert that something didn't seem right. Part of me was still giving him the benefit of the doubt though.

Out of the blue, he attacked me and tried to rape me! I punched him as hard as I could in his face. So hard, in fact, it hurt my hand so I knew it must have hurt him too. I ran out to my car and he ran after me, but I was a runner so he was no match for my speed. But when I tried to open the car door, he reached in to grab me. I struggled and fought with him, I managed to get inside the car and closed the door. He managed to open my door and in the chaos, he slammed the door on my left foot. I drove out of that parking lot as fast as I could, the car door still open, with my injured foot and bloody leg, to meet my friend.

We went straight to the police to tell them what had happened. They started an investigation and told me, there were no surveillance cameras outside or inside that particular hotel, which in their opinion was why the hotel was chosen.

This man had carefully planned the entire thing, the agent, the hotel with no cameras, the studio name, the production company, everything. He was a predator! I called the studio he pretended to be employed by and told them what had happened. Their lawyer got in touch with me immediately asking for all the details. They were very concerned because these people had used their name for the scam and they did all they could to help me.

As I found out through the studio, this was not even a project they were working on. I am not mentioning the studio or names because I am only sharing this experience so other up-and-coming actors can understand that there are these types of scams, and to be aware and to always trust your intuition.

Three years later my friend told me the man who I was attacked by was on the news. I asked her what happened to him and she told me the police were now looking for him as he had done this to someone else.

This is the art of an experienced con man; they know just enough to seem believable. I knew there was something wrong when I saw no trailers on what was supposed to be a movie set so thankfully, my guard was already up.

We don't know if he was ever really caught but my point is that there are always scams and people pretending to be what they are not. In my case, I was lucky because I drove my own car and took a friend with me, so he was not successful in raping me, but I probably gave him a black eye! He was nothing to do with the movie industry at all, he was just a con man, a rapist, and a predator, who knew just enough to appear plausible.

At the time, the police told me he had been doing this for a while, so obviously, they knew him from prior cases, yet he had not been caught yet. Although my experience was an isolated incident, we know things like this happened through the #MeToo movement and the Harvey Weinstein conviction.

Chapter 15:

The Cost of Early Success

When success comes too early, it is seldom appreciated.
— *Blanca Blanco*

Love it or hate it, the movie-making process is arduous and tiring with lots of downtime for lighting changes, new camera angles, sound issues, script corrections, and general production issues. These are normal and we take them in our stride as actors and actresses along with all the crew who also have to spend hours waiting around until these corrections are complete as the director wants them.

For me personally, I was just happy to have landed a role in a film and I saw it as a privilege to be there. But for some, their success was quite sudden when a movie or TV show suddenly hits and it becomes a big success. When overnight success like that happens, it can affect some who are not grounded.

I was surprised that for these few, having landed the role they dreamed of, their success made them difficult, "prima donnas" demanding things that normal people would never dream of. The movies they were working in, were made difficult for all involved because of their immature behavior. Their problems became everyone's problem. They are not grounded and their success is not in parallel with their maturity.

Many who behave badly are not even, what we call "A-Listers." Being an "A-Lister" is an achievement earned by our experience as a serious and convincing actor, who gradually moved up to be cast more prominently in lead roles that resulted in huge box office hits or were critically acclaimed.

One of the saddest things about this industry is some people's so-called "failures", lead them to take drugs or excessive alcohol as a means to deal with this "self-perceived," failure. By abusing drugs or alcohol, only serves as a band-aid. Sadly, they do not realize that this will not fix anything. Furthermore, drug abuse and mental health have a direct correlation with one another.

Some of whom I auditioned with, didn't even learn their lines so there was no chance at landing the role they were auditioning for. Others who landed the part didn't spend the time learning their lines either. To me, it is the same as learning how to do any job you are paid to do. In reality, acting is just another job and if the following direction, learning our lines, understanding the script, and developing a character, is the requirement, then we should all do that as well as we can. It's a team effort. We are all interconnected when filming a movie.

Keeping Politics Away from Movies

In this present day, with so much focus on politics, making political statements is a kiss of death in this business. One thing is certain, when, or if we do, it will lead to losing at least 50% of our fans or audience. I worked too hard to learn my skill to risk losing my career in this way. So I decline to make political statements.

I believe in free speech, but free speech also has consequences. If we, as actors or musicians, have a large following it is because of the roles we have played or the music we have made not because of our political views. We, therefore, have to think carefully about what we say in public. I have fans who are republicans, democrats, and independents and I respect them all. I am not to judge nor impose my beliefs onto others. We are all shaped and wired differently and it would be nice if we all had commonalities but in reality, we are all different coming from different backgrounds. That's the beauty of diversity.

One can't force change in someone else's behavior or traits as it's beyond our control. We can however influence others by providing encouragement and support or even through setting an example but we can't control anyone else's actions only our own.

Chapter 16:

Show Biz!

I find that the harder I work, the more luck I seem to have.
— *Thomas Jefferson*

When I first moved to Los Angeles to focus on my career, there were many of us, all starting out at the same time. The same faces always appeared at auditions and in various acting classes I attended. But now, after a few years, there are only one or two left that I still see around. This always brings it home to me that being one of a very few left from my original "crowd" proves how lucky I am to still be in the film industry. I often wonder what happened to them as they seemed to now be missing in action.

Before making my move to Los Angeles I did a lot of research so I understood how the system worked. I broke it down to its smallest unit so I was clear on what I needed to do to be successful in this industry. When I arrived in L.A., I did not have family or friends or anyone that was in the entertainment industry, so I had plenty of time for more reading and research. I then began taking the steps needed to begin in the entertainment industry by marketing myself. I understood what each role represented and how my team needed to be strongly interconnected in order to help achieve my artistic goals.

My goals were realistic; I already knew I could handle hard work, which is why I wanted to have my master's degree in place.

A big part of being in films is that everyone on the set is interdependent. We all do our part to the best of our ability to ensure the successful completion of the project.

The rewards are many as are the risks but I would have it no other way. It is a privilege to be part of this fantastic, magical, make-believe world. For me, in every way, it is a learning experience and as I said, I'm happy to be part of it.

A Tribute to Gordon Hunt

Success is often measured by what we leave behind. — Blanca Blanco

I feel honored Gordon Hunt was part of my journey. He coached me for 10 years and was not only my coach but he was also my friend and my mentor. While working together in his theater group he was full of energy and very caring to all the members. He was definitely a wonderful human being and his daughter Helen Hunt was such a sweetheart when she worked with us in our theater group. She was a phenomenal director and expected us to aim higher and higher. She always wanted us to reach higher than we expected. I loved that about her work as a director.

Gordon, was a successful producer, director, voice coach and has directed cartoons for television as well as sitcoms including *Mad About You*, which starred his daughter, the Oscar and Emmy-winning actress Helen Hunt.

I owe a great part of my success to Gordon Hunt his guidance and his amazing coaching skills, without which I may never have had the success I have in this tough business.

His advice put my mind in the right perspective regarding my auditions, he helped me get on the long ladder to my success. Gordon Hunt was "one of a kind" and I owe a huge thank you to him! Of course, I miss him, but his words, his teaching, and his coaching will stay with me along with all those who were fortunate enough to have been taught by him. Rest in peace Gordon and thank you for all you taught me.

Chapter 17:

Roles I like to Play

Playing a villain is more fun than playing a hero, but I am happy doing either role. — Blanca Blanco

I enjoy playing roles that have many layers with emotional changes in different scenes. I love dramatic roles, comedy, and I also love vulnerable roles. I have played a range of parts and I love the variety in all that I do.

Recently I played an amazing role in a movie. As of this writing, it is currently in post-production. In this movie, I was made up to be bald, which was a whole new experience for me as I love my hair (most women do) and I have included a photo of me completely bald for you to see!

I was a mom, who had special powers, and the special effects in the movie were phenomenal. My character had so much regret, anger, and rage, along with a compassionate, loving side, it was so much fun developing my role.

The most amazing part of being in movies is when after all the tiny pieces are interconnected, we see the beautiful cinematography. The real art of a movie director is just that. His or her vision sees how all these pieces fit together. Even with all this work, a movie or TV series can, in the end, flop! This I know is part of the risk we all take.

People have often asked me if, during filming, I can see if the movie is going to be a good one, or if, as I am working on it, I can see it may be crappy! The answer is no, not very often. This is more so in non-SAG authorized productions when I was starting out. I had to be in those non-SAG authorized movies as part of my, "apprenticeship," in order to get enough acting credits in different movies or shows to meet eligibility for my SAG membership.

I like to know who is directing an upcoming movie I have been cast in. I check the director's work on IMDb (Internet Movie Database), to see what they have worked on and see their style also. After I joined SAG, the professional level of the movies I auditioned for was at a much higher level. SAG does a lot behind the scenes to keep the business honest and professional. The hours we work, the crew, the staff it is all part of what SAG does.

In the beginning, just like anyone else, I accepted almost any role so I could gain experience and also eventually have enough credits to join SAG. The work of a casting director is to match us for the part we will audition for and a good casting director can make or break a movie.

I love playing dramatic roles because these are nothing like me in real life. In real life, I am definitely NOT dramatic. I strive to live a stress-free life – *without drama!* I enjoy playing a strong woman as that is how I see myself. My past has made me strong and I like who I am.

My Award

I won Best Supporting Actress in a film shot in Detroit called, *Betrayed.* It was based on a true story and I loved playing the villain. It was the first time I had been cast in this way. The role was exciting since it was not at all like the real me but like an alter ego and believe me I was a badass!

The movie was based on human trafficking and I loved, being cast as a tough, fierce, courageous female! I think that may even have been one of the reasons I won the award because I loved the role I played.

Self-Tape

Many times a casting director will request that I make a "self-tape video" to be submitted for an upcoming role. The "self-tape" is a personalized audition pulled from the script, instead of personally going in for the audition. I made the tapes at a professional studio to ensure the finished tape was the best quality I could get in order to have the best chance for a callback. These self-tapes were perfect for doing auditions during the Pandemic since I could just send them my auditions without the risk of getting COVID-19.

Additionally, I could study the part and do multiple takes then select the one that I am happy with. I always want to send in the work that I feel best represents me. The downside is that I have no way of meeting and seeing the casting director, producer, or director's face after my audition.

All in all, the self-tapes allow me to show my best side for the role. Luckily, I was able to do this from home.

During the pandemic, several of the studios sent me gift baskets to enjoy while watching movies and being stuck at home. They were so sweet to think of me and I thanked them all for their thoughtfulness. They made me feel so very special and their kindness deeply touched my heart.

Chapter 18:

Preparing for the Red Carpet

By failing to prepare, you are preparing to fail. — Benjamin Franklin

People have often asked me about the Red Carpet and what I do to get ready. My preparation for these events begins one month before and, in some cases, even before that. For me to be fully prepared for the Red Carpet my routine is to do the following:

❖ Cardio and weight training at least 5x week.
❖ Increase vegetables and lean protein, this is easy for me since I eat often and nearly always healthy foods.
❖ Drink plenty of water; the rule is to divide your weight by 2 and what it equals is what you need in ounces of water daily.
❖ Hydrate, Hydrate, Hydrate. No alcohol.
❖ Steam room (if possible). This helps with skin tone and suppleness.

Then a couple of days before the event I begin my more direct routine, nails, spray tan, facials, hair treatments, body scrubs.

Red Carpet Day!

I usually get up around 6 am to begin my "on the day" routine. Believe it or not, I am an early bird. I love waking up early so I can make my day productive (there are never enough hours in the day). I always begin with my exercises and eating a well-balanced breakfast. My team arrives soon after and I begin my "Red Carpet" routine. Hair and makeup usually take over 3 hours to complete. I take lots of selfies to share with fans while my hair and makeup are being done. I also do a WhatsApp chat with my family and friends to keep them posted on the progress since they were also involved in the planning. As a rule, no matter what the event may be, I try to have a backup outfit — *especially for a Red Carpet event.*

The last time, as I was getting ready to go to the Oscars, the zipper broke, and before you go thinking "Hey Blanca, lose some weight!" That was not the issue. It happens with zippers and one has to be prepared to go from Plan A to B to C. So, for me, attention to detail is what it is all about. I work carefully on my Red Carpet look.

Before every event, I keep my fashion designers informed and I send them photos. I want them to be pleasantly surprised at the final, "look" we have created. This is important as I always want to show them, how I look wearing their creations and you can see some of these beautiful creations later in my book. One of my strong assets is communication. I like to keep the designer and the rest of my team updated on the progress. Teamwork is important to me because every department contributes to the final look.

The Legal Side of the Red Carpet

Sometime before the event, the contractual obligations are completed. This happens for every event I am part of. I determine what I want to wear before the contract is drafted, which then includes my choice of clothes. We work as a partnership and our contract includes pay, performance, specifics of the clothes and in particular, it covers the dress they are going to provide me. When it is a high-profile event or an award show, the contracts become challenging because of narrowing down the designer I want to wear. That's a fun process for me though, deciding what type of look or vibe I want to display. Sometimes I make my own designs as I did for the Oscars and the Golden Globes, two years in a row. One of the outfits I designed is shown here in my book and another is on the back cover.

As I begin my walk, which can take 45 minutes or more to be photographed and to do interviews. People have often asked me if I am nervous at these highly publicized events. I don't get as nervous as I did in the beginning. Experience is a wonderful thing, I work on the things that are in my control, like organizing and preparing my presentation. The butterflies in my stomach are there, but they are happy butterflies. This makes me appreciate the experience. Feeling a bit vulnerable, now and then, leads to self-discovery and growth.

Of course, there is the pressure at the event. It's not just about the glamorous side but equally important is the business side. I enjoy the adrenalin rush of the press line, and I also love seeing the high number of placements in well-known magazines.

All of this attention to detail makes the designer and his (or her) team happy. Going viral is a beautiful feeling, and in the end, all the hard work turns into a very rewarding feeling. At the end of the night, when I arrive at my hotel, I change into my more comfortable clothes, then I go for a pizza and a glass of Sauvignon Blanc wine!

The Red Carpet — Moscow

In 2018, I was invited to the Moscow International Film Festival as an American actress to participate in the festival by watching films, attending workshops, and other various meetings. I also had Red Carpet appearances while there. This time, I was feeling anxious because I thought the Russian media didn't know me. I thought to myself, *what if they don't photograph me and I am wearing millions in Chopard jewelry and top Russian fashion designer, Igor Gulyaev's— because they don't know my name!* In this case, the pressure was adding up before heading to the Red Carpet. My objective is to always have strong placements. However, as soon as I arrived, I was relieved that many of the photographers knew who I was and were calling out to me. I was surprised that they even knew my name.

While in Russia, I was working and representing several different brands. We hope the brands we represent will go viral and take off, as that is a success for all of us. At that event, I was wearing jewelry by Chopard, worth $12 million for the entire 2 weeks. I was well protected by my two bodyguards while I was wearing these expensive jewelry items! It was in Moscow where I met the daughter of the original owner of *Chopard*, her name is Caroline Scheufele. She told me she loved how I wore her designs and said she would like me to represent her jewelry line in the future. This meant a lot to me since it showed all my preparations were well worth the effort.

While we were at the Cannes Film Festival this year, in 2021, Caroline and I were seated next to each other in the theater and that was quite a surprise for both of us, we laughed and caught up. It's always fun to meet people I have become acquainted with at these events.

After 5 years, as an actress and fashionista, I began to get my own headlines, which was a slow process. I have now been to the Oscars 5 times and the Golden Globe awards 6 times. Staying relevant is the key in my industry. This is important in this business as it is so easy to be forgotten.

After I was photographed, at a private event with Brad Pitt, the papers were full of gossip about Brad and me. The gossip was of course, not true but that's the nature of my business, and having my name attached to Brad Pitt in several articles, was not bad either! In fact, I had the biggest crush on him as a teen, one of the most handsome men in the world not to mention a phenomenal actor.

When I was being interviewed on these Red Carpet events by the press, and when my interviews aired or were written up into editorials, they often went viral — *the power of hard work, being true to myself, and of course, a bright smile and beautiful clothes can't hurt!*

Chapter 19:

Deciding to Succeed

If we are not challenged, then there is no growth. Experience is never wasted time. — Blanca Blanco

I have been asked the question several times, "How do you measure your success?" My success is not measured in "things," or "possessions."

So, when I think about measuring my success, it's none of the things most people think about. For me it's self-growth. Every year I give myself personal growth targets that I strive to reach, before the end of each year, to improve myself. There are many self-improvement actions I undertake, like my auditions, acting, training workshops, PR, film work, or my modeling.

It is the work we put into what we are trying to accomplish, that will give us the best chance to achieve our success in the end. Perception of personal success is different for each of us. So, what success means for me, is to achieve all the things I had set out to accomplish.

Personal growth for me is very important and it is the summary of all the pieces I place as my objectives, each year, from which I measure my growth and hence my success. I never place an objective as a "thing" but rather the actions I plan to undertake, in order to rise to where I want to be.

I decided to set my personal goals when I was back home in Washington State living in that garage and later in the trailer. I thought about it every single night and I made myself focus on hard work as a means of getting away from my humble beginnings. I had a burning desire to, *break the mold,* as a woman whose family immigrated to this country from Mexico. I didn't want to be merely a statistic. If I was going to break the mold as I saw it, I would have to work extremely hard to make this happen.

This is why for two reasons self-growth is so important to me. Firstly, it is how I measure my success, and, secondly, it is what enables me to *continue* to *break the mold.*

Setting My Goals

An example of planning for my success is that I would set one of my goals as doing a certain number of activities. I always set my goals at the beginning of the year. Part of this process is for me to set the number of things I specifically planned to do.

It may seem to you that my goals are little more than New Year's resolutions, but I don't see them as just New Year's Resolutions. I think carefully about what to include in my personal growth plan and for these to be measured with my actions. When one wants to develop new habits or new skills one must practice the new behavior at least 10 times in order for it to become a habit. So I patiently keep working at it until it is achievable, it takes time but is NOT impossible.

Every year my goals change but for example, they may include having a workout routine, eating healthy, taking several acting workshops to enhance my skills, increasing my auditions, updating my headshots, and booking a minimum number of films (a wish list) for the upcoming year.

Some of my goals may be out of my control, like the number of auditions I hope to do, or the number of confirmed film roles I may land, but this doesn't mean I can't at least set my goals. I also do a weekly "to do" list incorporating some of my goals for the year as a way to measure that I'm working towards it on a weekly basis.

From where I was, living in that tiny garage with my family and then moving into the trailer, I am proof that setting goals, for a step-by-step gradual success, works — *and it works well*. I encourage all who read my book to try this. It doesn't matter how small, how few, or how seemingly uninteresting these individual goals are, you envision your success in achieving them, one by one. If you try it, then achieving each goal is in itself very motivating. Also, remember any action you take is 100% better than taking no action. For example, taking a 5-minute walk is 100% better than not taking one at all! I don't mean to simplify this, but in reality, to me, it is that simple.

I did this all through school, and while in university with my course work. Without personal goals, we are not able to reach our success and if this is the case, we cannot imagine how successful any of us could be. I strongly believe it is better to say I tried and I failed than to look back and say I wish I would have done that. The gains from winning or losing contribute to the experience and personal growth.

By not measuring our self-growth, and setting goals, there could be regrets later in life. Changes can happen at any age, as we all understand, but what I am saying is that you could have had more time to enjoy the changes if they were made sooner than later.

On a positive note, when circumstances change, one learns and one can gain stronger adaptability skills. This is a skill that can apply in many areas of our lives. For example, during the COVID-19 pandemic, which was not in any of our goals, we learned to navigate through the new changes and rearranged our goals.

Try it and see for yourself! Just set yourself a few goals that could be something to do that you have been putting off. When you pair your goals with actions, then you have a sense of accomplishment.

Always remember a baby goes from crawling to walking, from walking to running. You take one step, then another; falling, getting back at it, and the accomplishments progress until that baby can run. So, let's stay positive and motivated!

Chapter 20:

My Volunteer Work

The best way to find yourself is to lose yourself in the service of others. — Mahatma Gandhi

In a magazine interview, I was once asked about my volunteer work with the *L.A. Step Up* program and the Los Angeles Mission. I began volunteering with *Step Up* because I believed their mission statement resonated strongly with me. They work with girls in underserved communities to help them reach their potential by encouraging them to be confident and focus on a career. I studied poverty and looked into the reasons why poverty continues with the children who are born into poverty. I am a strong believer that education is key to breaking the cycle of poverty and that coming from poverty does not have to dictate your future. I believe anyone can overcome and achieve goals with tenacity, dedication, and commitment and while it can be challenging, it's always possible as I proved with my own education.

During the interview, I also told them *that* I hope to serve as a role model for successfully turning barriers into challenges and then into success. Staying focused while setting myself on the path I chose for my life was the result of turning barriers into successes. I gave myself "permission" to accept my situation with my childhood and to focus on growing and moving forward. As I said in the last chapter, I achieve this for myself by making step-by-step goals to achieve success.

I have also volunteered with Los Angeles Mission for over eight years now. I volunteer during holidays, Thanksgiving, Christmas, and Easter, to serve hot meals to those in need because I know, first hand, how much it can mean to someone to have that. To many of the people we serve meals to, this is the only proper meal they will get for a while. I love to see everyone's smiles and to be able to help however I can. For me, it's a way of giving back to the community. Being of service to others is my number one principle and this will never change. My own family's poverty left an indelible impression on me that I never want to repeat and I don't want this for others, so I try to help in whatever way I can.

Whenever we enter the Skid Row area, to go into the L.A. Mission shelter, seeing the gigantic lines of people waiting to be served a hot meal brings me to tears every time. We have a higher level of homelessness and people experiencing poverty in L.A. than most other places — especially now since the Pandemic. I remember one day when I was a sophomore in college a homeless man was holding a sign asking for money for food. I was so hungry and was on my way to Subway and it made me so sad to see this homeless man so I gave him the 5 bucks I had on me, which was meant for my meal. I have a soft heart when it comes to seeing a person struggling and if I can help, I help. A colleague was with me in the car and said, "You know he is probably just gonna buy beer or drugs." I replied, "The action that he takes is his choice, not mine, and is out of my control." I felt good helping someone who needed it.

If I could leave one message behind for my readers. I would say to remember that while on your journey, there will always be obstacles, so choose to use those experiences to change your thinking by simply seeing the obstacles as challenges. Doing so will help you build a positive outlook and drive your goals forward. Lastly, always believe in yourself because if you don't, how do you expect other people to believe in you? I am a strong believer in each of us managing our own destiny since we are given all the tools we will need to succeed, in our lives, if we choose to.

I worked hard at "breaking the mold" following my own childhood, living in poverty. According to all the statistics, poverty could have led my siblings and me to continue in poverty if we were to become a "usual statistic." But our situation was nothing that I was responsible for or anything I could change at the time.

There are many organizations to help, many of which are free. So never accept that you are not able to change your future. You can do this!

Chapter 21:

Typecast in Social Standing

If you really want to do something, you'll find a way. If you don't, you'll find an excuse.—Jim Rohn

Part of my success was my training, to achieve my degrees in psychology and social work, which led me to see firsthand what living in poverty can lead to. Studies showed that children living in poverty are, for the most part, destined to remain in poverty. This affects all children no matter what race they are.

I wanted to learn how to break out of my poverty "mold" and open new doors. Some people's perception of Latinos here in the U.S. is to believe we are, for the most part, roofers, kitchen staff, gardeners, cleaning staff, and other similar worker profiles. We work in these fields, but we are also doctors, lawyers and we are also in many other professional fields. I wanted to prove that we have the ability, the ideals, the drive, and the motivation to achieve whatever we wish to achieve if we are given the tools to try, and I was determined to succeed!

When growing up, I realized it was difficult for my family and me to communicate with the neighbors or at the grocery store, because we didn't speak English. This was challenging and even though I was learning English at school, my parents worked in a Spanish-speaking environment and were not exposed to the English language as much as my siblings and I, so that made it harder for them to learn and be able to communicate in English. I know now, that we had limited opportunities because of it. Once I learned the language, I had more opportunities and was able to integrate into the community without losing my own identity and culture.

This was my experience growing up and seeing how having limitations in language worked against us and many opportunities closed because of it. I am still learning English to this day. One goal that I made for myself, was to learn more English besides what I learned in school. So I bought a dictionary and tried to learn 1 word a day. Imagine, that's 365 new words a year!

Our school, in Washington State, was a great school where my siblings and I excelled. They helped us to learn English and to place us on equal footing in our classes as soon as possible. My parents couldn't speak English when we were young, but they could understand and communicate a few words. However, years later, my mother enrolled at the Community College of Spokane's Institute for Extended learning where she began to learn English. She was very proud to show me her student ID and loved sharing what she was learning there. Then both of my parents passed their citizenship test with hard work and lots of practice. It was one of their happiest days, especially for my mom, to receive their U.S. Citizenship. Mom was so happy! Even her teachers helped her prepare for the citizenship exam. It's never too late to try to improve your life and I have included a photo of my mom with her U.S. Citizenship certificate.

The American Dream
One of Mami's proudest moments in her life, is photographed here with the judge, when she became an American Citizen. Here she is with a big smile on her face, having learned English and all about the American Constitution! We were all so proud of you Mami.

Chapter 22:

My Love for Cooking

Simple ingredients, prepared in a simple way – that's the best way to take your everyday cooking to a higher level.
— José Andrés

Of all the bad things associated with 2020 and the COVID-19 pandemic, was that going to the shops or eating in restaurants became impossible for a while. This was the beginning of me cooking more at home. Before the COVID-19 pandemic, I often went out to restaurants because we were on the move the whole time, and eating out was not even a thought, it was for convenience in our fast-paced lives. Living in Malibu, when all my meetings were in L.A. at all times of the day and night, often with back-to-back appointments, meant I grabbed a bite on the go and arrived back home late. But now all this had changed and changed for a long period of time, so it meant I had to change my style of living.

I love eating healthy foods, but only vegetables and salads for a year, while this pandemic was still going strong, was out of the question for me.

I started cooking a lot more than I did before. It was not that I couldn't cook. I often helped my mother in the kitchen. Cooking with my mom was fun, and I loved it. I also realized that I am a good cook and found it satisfying. Cooking was another thing I could check off my list of personal goals and achievements.

I love cooking all sorts of dishes, Chicken Alfredo, teriyaki chicken pasta, seafood, plus all the dishes my mother taught me to cook. I love making soups too, and I love preparing and interesting salads. My cooking was not as you would say conventional in that I do not get a recipe book out and follow it to create a well-known dish. I go out to the grocery store pick up all I think I will need and start cooking.

Much of what I learned was from helping and watching my mom cook for us. I would watch her make homemade tortillas from scratch and she was so passionate about making sure all tortillas were in the same shape and looked beautiful. She put so much of her heart and soul into her cooking. I loved when she made Pozole Stew. It was so delicious and the house smelled so good, not to mention her homemade salsas were the best too. I have a lot of experience cooking Mexican food, which of course, I naturally love! Mami was a great cook and could make something from almost nothing. When we were growing up, she was used to making the most of what we could afford and we looked forward to enjoying what she had created. Mom was an expert at creating her dishes and cooked for dad, who never went hungry.

Keep in mind we always encouraged mom to eat heart-healthy foods because she had diabetes and hypertension. We all enjoyed eating Mexican food, which made things a little more challenging nutrition-wise.

I am sharing a couple of her signature handwritten dishes below, that she would make on special occasions.

Canon de de Puerco y Papa

hajo - Pimienta comino sopapera los taco
Sitomate comino oregano hajo sopapera
sal al gusto

Birria de Borrego
Para un Borrego
2 Cabesa de hajos 1½ de comino
10 Pimientas 3 clavos de olor
2 tasos de vinagre

Salsa para la Birria
1 Paquetes de chiles Pusa 2 hajos
comino Poca vinagre

Birria d Res   4 Libras de Corn.
1 cabesa de Ajo   2 clavos de olor
16 Pimientas 1 cuchara sopera de cominos
1 tasa de vinagre   sal al gusto

Mom's handwritten recipes.
English translation on the next page.

Mago's Birria Stew Recipe
Pork meat and potatoes

Add 2 cloves garlic, 10 crushed pepper balls, 1 ½ tablespoon cumin, diced tomatoes, oregano, salt to taste, to create tasty juice for taco meat, 2 cups of vinegar, marinate meat.

Beef Birria   4 pounds of meat
26 clove of garlic
26 crushed pepper balls,
1 tablespoon of cumin
1 cup of vinegar
Salt to taste

* * * * *

Mago's Tamales Recipe

*Soak the corn husks
  Prepare the filling - cook chicken or pork

*To prepare the salsa, boil 2 tomatillos, 2 tomatoes, 3 garlic cloves, half spoon pepper, half an onion, 4 guajillo chilies. After all is boiled, blend it. Shred meat and mix it with the salsa

*Make masa dough, mix masa flour, baking powder, salt, cumin, some oil, mix all until creamy

*Assemble the tamales. Lay corn husk, add ¼ cup of dough spread, add salsa meat in center. Close corn husk like a burrito with open end.

*Cook- add water to the stove-top on don't fill it past steamer pot, place them standing up and then cover tamales with the remaining of corn husk, boil for about 1 hour
  *Enjoy!

Cooking and celebrating Thanksgiving 2020 with
mom, —*COVID-19 style.*

Chapter 23:

The Woolsey Fire

It is sometimes how we deal with unforeseen events that define us. — Blanca Blanco

My first sight of the "fluffy" white cloud I saw from PCH...I had no idea when I took this selfie, what devastation it would cause, but it made me nervous as you can see...

The Beginning of the Woolsey Fire

The Woolsey fire that occurred in November 2018 was one of the worse experiences in my life. It came out of nowhere and changed all my previous thinking.

I woke up around 6 am on November 9th, 2018, and got ready for my day. It was an ordinary bright, warm and sunny day of the type we always have in Malibu. John, my significant other, had major surgery the day before and was in bed that morning, still a little groggy, from the anesthetic he had received. The weather outside was, as usual, sunny and warm, with blue skies. There was a white fluffy cloud, that looked like my bunny, Star-Star, but it was further inland from me.

On that morning, I happened to notice a U-Haul truck outside a neighbor's home, which was leaving as I started my car. I had several business meetings that day, so I left the house and drove onto the PCH (Pacific Coast Highway). As I turned onto the highway, I could see that the traffic was almost at a standstill, which I thought was because of an accident further up the road.

Unfortunately, that type of slow traffic can be normal in Malibu since we have many accidents on the PCH. I didn't think too much about it as I had plenty of time to get to my 9 am meeting. But this time the PCH was like a parking lot as I entered the highway.

Anyway, I knew I still had a couple of hours before my first meeting. I thought I would eventually pass the accident site (still believing it *was* an accident), and after that, I would make up time. My drive to L.A. usually took around 45 minutes. But the PCH was still not moving.

I called a friend as my car slowly crawled past her house, and said, "Hey I'm just passing your house but the traffic is standing still here on PCH." I added, "Hey check out that big cloud by your house." She said, "Hey cool, thanks for letting me know I'll go outside and check it out."

Anyway, as I was sitting in my car and not moving, I tried the radio, switching from station to station, but there was nothing on the news about an accident.

I had only moved about half a block in 40 minutes, so I thought I would turn around and take a different route, and get off the PCH. I decided to take the Canyon route as I still had time. But I had this weird feeling something was very wrong, yet there was nothing on the news and I thought if the traffic is this very bad it must be for a reason. My bad feeling was getting worse as I looked at the high volume of cars and I was thinking, if this was just an accident there surely wouldn't be this many cars! I also saw so many trailers, carrying horses, which was unusual for that time of year.

So, I turned around and went back to my neighborhood. As I arrived, I saw one of my neighbors putting his belongings in his car. I spoke to him as he was making many trips to and from his house loading his car and I asked him if he knew if there was a bad traffic accident causing all the cars on PCH to stop. Then I got the shocking news as he said, "Haven't you heard, we have all been evacuated!" That moment was the first I had heard about the wildfire heading directly towards our neighborhood.

Not understanding my neighbor's comment, I asked him, "Why is that? What's happened?" I was looking over to my home and now realizing that my entire neighborhood was so very quiet like a ghost town. It had never been like this before. I was beginning to get scared when he told me, "There's a huge wildfire heading our way." I said, "But the sky is so blue, where is it?" He said, "It's coming from behind, pointing to the hills further inland from where we were standing and it's headed our way." He continued to load his car as we were talking.

143

He told me the evacuation order had been given 3 hours ago at 6 am! Because I am an early riser, it saved my life. They supposedly announced on TV that morning but because I was rushing to leave, I didn't have time to watch the news. I wondered why didn't they have loudspeakers or a siren, or a reverse 911 call?

I am still shocked that none of the police or firefighters had come door to door or had used loudspeakers in and around our neighborhood to warn us about the fire. There was nothing on the radio, so what were we supposed to do if we didn't know? As for John and I, we knew nothing about it. No firemen were around and no police were around. Nothing made sense. There was plenty of time from around 6 am to warn us even door to door. I found out later that fire stations in other townships always have big sirens to warn of tornadoes, or floods, or impending danger. If our local fire department had used this, we certainly didn't hear it! The Point Dume fire station is only half a block away from our house so we all would have heard it.

I hurried back to my house, ran upstairs, and tried to wake John up to warn him we had to leave the house immediately. But John was not waking up! By this time, we only had around 10 minutes to leave and take whatever we could get in our car.

I was becoming frantic and had to slap John around his face to wake him up as time was running out. He finally awoke saying "Wha, wha, wha's going on, you slapped me!" I said, "John, we have to go right now we have to leave the house immediately, there's a huge wildfire which will be here in only 10 minutes!" He snapped awake and finally got his act together. We quickly grabbed our legal documents, passports, social security cards, birth certificate, and other documents that we knew we might need.

We each packed a small overnight bag and next I had to get Star-Star my pet bunny! Well, so much for that, she was running all over

144

the place and refused to let me catch her. She was out in the garden or in the room and where she could move around freely. But as I was trying hard to get her, she was now panicked and kept running away. The time was running out but I was not going to leave her behind. John and I were trying to grab her and the more we tried the more panicked she became. We finally threw a blanket over her and picked her up to get her into the car as quickly as we could. We put her into her pet carrier and placed her on the seat next to me. Star-Star was only 4 oz at that time, but she was a very fast bunny!

It's funny, have you ever thought about what you would take in an emergency if you only had a few minutes to pack? Although John and I were busy grabbing a few things, we were also in denial about the seriousness of our situation and I didn't take many belongings. People said afterward, "Oh you didn't take your jewelry, that's the first thing I would have taken." I thought to myself, "Just shut up! You weren't there." I only took what I could grab. When it happens to you and it is for real, you don't immediately start to make a list, you just grab everything you can.

I knew I would need my legal documents as I had the Latin Grammys coming up the following week, and I would be traveling to Marrakesh, Morocco. I had some beautiful designer dresses, that French designer Christophe Guillarme, sent for me to wear at the Grammy's in Las Vegas, Nevada. I grabbed a designer dress I thought I might need. But I didn't take the heels I was going to wear with it. I quickly grabbed a few day clothes as well and stuffed them into my bag. Usually hanging around Malibu, I wear "Lulu Lemon Apparel," fitness clothes, but still casual wear. I also grabbed my UGGs. because I thought we'll probably be back tonight or tomorrow.

I was still in denial hoping the fire would not reach my house. I thought as I was leaving my house and looking around my neighborhood everything looks fine the chances are very slim, we will even be hit because the sky was so blue, the sun was out and everything was calm.

But in fact, everything was just too quiet. Not even a single bird was in the sky. John wanted to stay and talk to the firefighters. The trouble was there weren't any around yet and I told him he was not a firefighter and he should leave with me and not hang around. We agreed to meet at our local gas station. We each drove a car; in a few minutes, I would call him to tell him I had arrived.

As I left the house, I looked up at the sky and sniffed the air but there was no smell of smoke around. I did notice that now the white fluffy cloud that reminded me of Star-Star, my bunny, was beginning to look a little darker and bigger.

As I started to drive my car onto the PCH, I didn't know which direction I should go. If I turned left, it would take me to Santa Monica and if I turned right, it would take me to Oxnard. The slow traffic, that I was originally stuck in, was headed toward Santa Monica.

There was still no news as I skipped through the saved channels on my radio and I still didn't know where the fire was coming from. One thing I did know was that the traffic on PCH going to Santa Monica was still not moving. As I was deciding what to do, many of the cars were turning around headed away from Santa Monica. So I made my choice to turn right and head to the gas station where I could ask people there for more information while getting gas.

Armageddon at the Gas Station

When I got to my local Chevron station, I couldn't believe my eyes, people were bumping into each other's cars and there was mayhem there. People were shouting at each other, fighting for the pumps, pushing and shoving each other to get to the next available pump. It took me almost an hour to finally get to a pump as there were so many cars lined up there now.

I was terrified at seeing what was unfolding right in front of me. Ordinary people, some of who I recognized, had now become very aggressive, angry, fighting each other. I was feeling a panic attack coming on as what I was seeing was making me more and more scared. Now I was seeing the previously white clouds becoming black and it was getting darker. There were flakes of ashes floating gently, like snowflakes in the sky above, blown by a wind, probably caused by the fire heading our way. A couple of people pushed in front of me at the pump and yanked the gas nozzle right out of my hands. This was now a very dangerous place to be and it was "survival of the fittest." I am not aggressive at all and these men were driving big trucks, pushing in front of everyone so I could do nothing.

I was calling and calling John but there was no response, nothing at all, which made me scared for him as I had no idea if he had decided to stay or if he had left. I was alone!

I had enough gas in my tank to go another 80 miles, so I could easily make it as far as Camarillo. But with the traffic moving so slowly, what if I run out of gas? People are never going to stop to pick up a stranger. Things just kept getting worse in my mind. An elderly lady was crying as her husband came back from paying for gas in the office. As they were next to me, I asked them which way were they going? I still didn't know which direction the fire was coming from and time was running out. They told me if I go towards Oxnard there is less traffic.

They said at least you can get through if you head that way, the traffic was moving, though slowly and bumper to bumper, but it was nevertheless moving. I now knew whichever direction I took, could mean life or death for me. This was now a very real and very serious situation. Anyway, finally, it was my turn at the pump, when just then the guy working at the gas station, who I knew and who usually filled my car, came out of the store. I could see the look in his eyes full of fear as he approached me. He told everyone, "No more gas, we've just run out of gas!" The anger and aggressiveness of people yelling after hearing the news were scary to witness and I was in complete shock.

This was the worst news and I thought, *Oh my gosh! What do I do now?* I didn't know what to do but one thing I did know, I couldn't stay there.

I left the gas station where I had been waiting now for over an hour while the fire was now moving very close to where we were. On my left was the Pacific Ocean and on my right was the fire now heading very fast towards the coast. PCH was running parallel to the coast and the fire was moving in on the highway.

I decided to head right towards Camarillo and I had now entered into the slowly moving line of traffic. After a few minutes of driving, I could not believe what I was seeing and I couldn't turn around anymore. The fire was very close and I could see ashes sparks and flames up on the hill blowing down towards all the cars in my slowly moving line of traffic.

More sparks are now flying through the air as I moved slowly in the line of traffic. My window had become so hot, from the heat now all around me, I couldn't touch it! The fire had moved relentlessly forward and was inching next to the road as far as I could see. PCH is only one lane in either direction, so if even one car stopped or broke down, we were all going to be in very serious trouble and could even die. At that moment, there was a beach, I was thinking if the traffic stops, I would have to run down to the ocean and if the fire reached there, I would probably drown.

Looking at the ocean, in the state I was in, as I was driving slowly, hoping I would make it ok, I remembered that I almost drowned in California when I was younger. I was rescued by a biker otherwise if not for him I would not be here. I was hoping and praying I would make it past the fire as either way it didn't look good for me at that moment. I didn't know if I was going the right way! My anxiety was out of control but there was one thing I could do and that was to keep moving forward.

Chapter 24:

To Fry or Drown

Trust your intuition; it's there for a reason. — Blanca Blanco

As I was driving so slowly, I tried to call my family, John's family, and my friends, anyone would do, but there was no signal. I kept trying and finally got through to a friend, I told her where I was, what was happening and asked her to call my mom if anything happened or I didn't make it through. I asked her to tell my mom that I loved her. I was crying in my car at the thought of how bad my situation had become. My mom watches the news in the mornings and if she knew about the fire, she would be so worried for my safety. I also knew, if she knew about it, she would be calling me, like she did when there was a small earthquake in my area. She always called to check on me, so that anxiety kept building up of not being able to reach her.

I was now personally dealing firsthand with the panic and despair, that I had helped my patients deal with when I was working in hospice care. Of course, it was now at a different level, but with similar emotions. I was alone and I had to try hard to stay positive but it was very difficult for me to stay calm at that moment. I tried hard to think of what my mom would always tell me, stay positive and tell yourself you are going to be okay. She would always say to me, "Que Dios te bendiga (*God Bless you*)", in every conversation or interaction. This was her way of giving me her blessing.

Anxiety

I thought to myself, here I am facing a possible life or death situation while my mom was probably preparing lunch! Stupid as that thought was, it made me smile and broke my feeling of foreboding at my predicament. But the feeling of anxiety and panic was now getting worse as the line of traffic moved so slowly, at a snail's pace, though the fire that was now leaping over the hill and coming towards the road we were all driving on. Looking to my right the silhouette of the hills was now lit orange, with the glowing fire all across the entire hillsides, for as far as I could see. I put Star-Star on my lap and was stroking her snow-white fur, as much to calm me down as it was, for her.

I was taking deep breaths to reduce my stress level as I could feel the panic attack increasing. The only other time I had experienced a panic attack was when I was boarding a connecting flight to L.A. It was to be a 3-hour flight. As I boarded, I knew I was feeling panicky. There was no way I could trust myself to sit in the aircraft for 3 hours and deal with it. So I told the stewardess just before they were about to close the door that I had to get off the plane.

* * * * *

Back then, it came on so suddenly, I thought I had a brain tumor or was having a stroke! I was so scared. Following that episode, I went to see my primary doctor. He told me after listening to my story of what had happened, that I had experienced a panic attack. After my doctor had told me that my blood work tests came back normal. I thought, *Thank God I don't have a tumor on my brain*, but I thought to myself, *how can that happen when I've got my life so organized?*

He told me anyone can get them but as long as they are not regular, which clearly mine were not, some medications can help. He recommended that I see a therapist who could definitely help me.

Following my meeting with the new doctor he wanted to prescribe Lorazepam, but I told him I didn't want Lorazepam. He told me he thought maybe I had a phobia against medication, which I didn't. I just didn't want to be dependent on anything, no matter what it was. That doctor didn't want to deal with me because I didn't want to take his recommended Lorazepam. To be clear, he recommended this to me after a 5-minute conversation. He knew nothing about me or my life.

I did fill the prescription and picked up the Lorazepam. I kept the Lorazepam with me and I only used it once or twice. I cut the tablet in half and half again as that was enough and I wasn't going to risk addiction. Yes, I was fearful of becoming dependent, but I kept the tablets, *just in case*.

Since that doctor was pushing medication, I told him I may feel better after I speak with someone else about my anxiety. I asked if he could recommend me to a therapist so I could work on a daily basis at learning the skills and tools I needed to get better. He looked at me strangely, like I was a difficult patient, and said alright, okay, and then he asked me to leave!

I liked seeing my therapist and told her I just didn't want to take the medication the doctor had prescribed, adding that I just was experiencing anxiety because I had my first panic attack and the fear of it happening again was giving me almost a daily anxiety. I went 3 times a week to meet with her. I also kept the medication in my purse, just in case I need it.

I am not against medication, but I feel that if there is something I can work on myself, like skills that can help to overcome the anxiety, then I prefer not to depend on a pill. After all, it will be me facing these attacks and I need to learn how to cope and manage them on my own. I knew medication only alleviated the symptoms. It was not a cure. I have never used any recreational drugs in my life. I was genuinely never interested in that or anything that is not healthy for my body or that would manipulate my mind.

* * * * *

Anyway, back to driving on the PCH. My panic attack is getting worse. I was shaking, sweating and my heart was racing. I felt I was not in control of anything around me. The heat was getting worse and the windows on my car were now so hot they were radiating heat inside the car. I turned the AC on as high as it would go, hoping it would not break down, working overtime to keep the car cool.

The flames were leaping up over my car so close to me now. Hot sparks and ashes were drifting all around my car. It was pitch black with smoke drifting and swirling in front and behind me. I had never in my life had such a feeling of complete despair. The fear of dying alone was racing through my mind.

Every time the convoy of cars stopped my heart rate rose and I felt I was going to die as I kept looking over to my right seeing the smoke and flames. I kept thinking of John and I had no idea where he was or if he was ok. I kept trying to call him but there was no signal, which made my feeling of being completely alone even worse.

I had to make myself go through a series of actions to center myself. So I focused on my hand on the steering wheel, my seat, the dash, and the gauges. I tried to stay in the "present" to eliminate the negative thoughts that would feed my anxiety. I could see the line of headlights of the line of cars behind me but they disappeared after only 2 or 3 cars because of the choking smoke that was blowing across the road which sometimes revealed more behind and in front of me but mostly only those few cars.

The traffic in front was moving slowly, too slowly, and the sky was now black, filled with flying sparks and ash. Even my headlights couldn't see through the darkness of the smoke all around me. I could only focus on the tail lights that I could just see, of the car in front and hope that I could keep moving, praying no one broke down. I could feel the heat now all over my car as I was making my way through the worst of the fire.

I was crying while trying to keep it all together, driving through, what was to me, a life-or-death situation. Even with my training in psychology, and attempting to use my skills to calm myself down, I couldn't help but think, over and over again, that I was going to die. I wondered if I may have made the wrong decision back when I got on the PCH after leaving my house. Yes, I did go toward the fire and there was a sense of regret there. But I saw that traffic going the other way towards Santa Monica was not moving at all, so at least I was moving even if it was very slow with stop and start driving. I was trying to justify my behavior and that was making it harder for me. The what-ifs and the maybes make things worse, and in reality, I was feeding the anxiety.

If I was to measure my level of anxiety, from 1 to 10 it was a level 10. As I moved further away from that gas station and all that had happened there, the fire was continuing to get worse. I had now been driving for 2 hours on the PCH. My anxiety continued to increase but I reminded myself, thinking *I am strong I can do this* and I kept thinking, *I must keep Star-Star safe*.

I was crying, I had panic, anxiety, dread, all those negative and debilitating feelings, along with the unknowns, like if the fire would get worse. *Would I survive?* All these thoughts fed my anxiety and even though I knew I was doing this; it was hard to rationalize things in my mind. I had to use the techniques, that I had learned in my therapy training and my therapy sessions, but now I had to use them on myself to help me through.

My heart rate was climbing and it felt like my chest would explode. Every time the cars stopped, I looked to the right to see if the flames would reach my car. I worked on deep breathing exercises and tried to focus on good thoughts instead of on what was happening around me. I said a prayer and imagined I was praying with my mom. She taught me to do daily prayers, and as I said them now, it gave me a sense of comfort. After the prayers, I knew I had two options, to either stay focused on my fear or focus on the positive; that I would soon be through this and be safe with Star-Star.

Changing my thought process was not as easy as I thought. A strange thing began to happen. My arms and my hands felt as heavy as lead weights and I struggled to keep them on the steering wheel. I was feeling like I was going to pass out. That was just the anxiety talking. Then I said to myself out loud, "Fuck this! I am better than this." I have overcome other fears before, so I can definitely overcome this fear.

I started focusing on breathing; deep, belly breathing so I would take deeper breaths while increasing oxygen to my brain so it calmed me down. I would breathe steadily while focusing on each part of my body. For example, I would start at my head, neck, chest, heart, arms, legs, ankles, all the way down, and then up again. This relaxation technique is very effective it has worked for me many times as it keeps me present in my body and my racing thoughts would reduce. Not to mention lowering my speedy heart rate. You can try this exercise yourself. You can be sitting down, standing up, in any situation or any position. The purpose is to keep you present in your body by focusing on deep breathing.

I was redirecting my thoughts, or "re-framing" trying to focus on the positive, not on everything that was going on around me and Star-Star. I worried every time traffic stopped and so I would take deeper breaths at each stop and that helped me stay calmer while at the same time my motivation to refuse to allow myself to panic was there. The reason I needed to be present in my body was because the anxiety was making me feel like I was going to pass out, but if I was in the present, I could focus on my breathing. One doesn't realize how strong we are until we are faced with traumatic situations.

All around me was chaos but I knew I was strong and I could and would, get through this. I tried to visualize what I would be doing when I got to Camarillo; go for a walk, call mom and hear her laughter, smell the fresh air that gave me a sense of hope. Having a sense of hope reminded me I had things to do in the future and gave me a sense of taking steps, actions, even small steps, things to look forward to.

Seeing the scared look on the faces of the drivers in the few cars that were coming the other way made it so real. My choices could affect many and could be deadly. A sense of responsibility came over me. I reminded myself that I am a healthy person and I have never passed out before. My fear was just the anxiety talking. Of course, the physical signs are there like racing thoughts, and feelings of despair, so I needed to start from there to calm myself down and stop this illogical thinking of "I'm going to pass out."

I had so much adrenaline rushing through my body. I started deep breathing and turned the AC up to full to make it cold in the car. It was important as I was only circulating the air already in my car and I was not bringing air from the heavily smoky air outside.

When I was having this particular anxiety attack, all my training went out of the window because my thoughts were racing at 100 miles per minute. I wasn't able to deal with one thing at a time, I was dealing with all emotions simultaneously.

We can have a positive outlook, we can also be strong. I am a strong and driven woman, but an anxiety attack can happen to anyone at any time. We are all human and when we have challenges, our body sends us reminders, that we need to pay attention to, so we can internally reduce our stress.

I continue to remind myself that anxiety will always be there. It is a constant. Those feelings must be managed or else they will eventually return to the surface and become harder to deal with.

Through my training, I was able to recognize the symptoms and try to manage them, which I knew I just had to do but at the same time, I was naturally scared. When we are in "panic" or, "anxiety" mode all logic goes out of the window! Well, I knew that was happening, so I had to find my inner strength to work harder at managing this and also to understand what I was feeling was very normal considering the situation I was in.

The car radio was fading in and out but when music was playing, I tried to focus on the words I could hear and started singing along with the music (Star-Star didn't seem to mind). It definitely helped and I grabbed Star-Star stroking and petting her to keep us both calm, telling her, *it's ok, it's ok*. Bunnies can feel human emotion. We had been a family for a while and I knew that she was depending on me. Star-Star felt every emotion I was feeling.

At that moment, I was at the mercy of the fire. Right now, I controlled nothing at all, I was completely at the mercy of whatever this fire would do, but however bad it was, I tried to remain hopeful that little Star-Star and I would not be swallowed up by these flames.

As I looked left to the ocean, I was surprised to see so many horses tied up on the beach. People had taken them there and I thought, "I hope and pray they all make it." Horses can move fast and seem to have a sense of which way to run away from danger, but these horses were tied up to the beach lifeguard tower. I was surprised to see some owners tying the horses to the tower and leaving them there like that. I thought, what if the fire gets near them how can they escape? I didn't want to judge as we were all were going through major stress, and doing the best we can, but it made me sad wondering if anything bad happens to the horses that were tied up, what could they do? In hindsight, where they were, may have been the safest place for them.

I finally left the PCH and got onto Las Posas Road, heading up to higher land and north and I was finally through the worst of the fire. I shouted to myself in my car, "I MADE IT!" I was calming down now and so happy that the Woolsey Fire had not claimed me and Star-Star. I had never felt this level of relief in my life before. Now I called my mom to tell her I was good and it was perfect timing because she said she was just watching the news and was going to call me because she was worried. I called everyone I could and was happy that I could finally get through. It was like a celebration that we had made it. I got through to John and found that he was somewhere behind me traveling on the same road.

All this happened while I was driving through the fire and it occurred in a time frame of only around three and a half hours, from the time I first learned from my neighbor that we had all been evacuated. But for me, it was the longest three hours of my entire life, for a drive that should have only been 20 minutes.

Chapter 25:

The Woolsey Fire — News Coverage

You woke up today, it's already a good day — Blanca Blanco

Despite all the trauma I suffered, I did make it through and so did John. I was now so happy that the worst was behind me, or so I thought! I was now in Camarillo where John and I finally met up at a gas station and went into a restaurant to watch TV. We both wanted to watch the news to see what had just happened because we still knew nothing at all about this fire.

My friend who I had called when I was first on the PCH had also taken the same route that John and I had taken. So, I called her to see that she was ok. She was ok and we arranged for her to meet us at the restaurant.

We all sat down together to watch the news of the fire. As we were watching it, I had no appetite for lunch. As we looked up at the TV, we could see our house, burning down in a huge fireball! We were seeing our beautiful home and all our belongings burning. We were shocked into silence! But as I watched my home burning, I couldn't help but think, *where are all the firefighters? Why are there none there, not even one?* I felt angry and frustrated as apparently other areas that were also burning were the priorities of our firefighters.

After many attempts to enter our neighborhood, a couple of weeks later, we were allowed to go in. The weeks of waiting felt like an eternity. We went back to see if there was anything left. There was very little, except one of my framed certificates. I have no idea how it made it without being completely destroyed. I have a photo of the certificate that I retrieved. It had been under the rubble, which probably saved it from being destroyed.

Looters

What made this entire experience even worse was that there were looters, all over our neighborhood looking for things we had left behind to steal. When we evacuated in such a hurry, we were most concerned about our safety, not what we were leaving behind.

I saw on breaking news that there were looters in our neighborhood and our residents were patrolling with guns. I wondered how the looters entered our neighborhood to steal from our homes when the roads were closed and residents were not allowed to enter at all.

Chapter 26:

My Destroyed Home

Most of what we own are just "things" we collect, as we are passing through. — Blanca Blanco

After a few days, I decided to see what damage had been done to our home. I carefully climbed the unsafe stairs, treading only on the edges of each step close to the wall, where it would be safer than the middle of each step on those that were left. I went into what was my bedroom, I looked around to see if any of my clothes could be saved. My once beautiful shoes were all ruined and every single pair was destroyed. I looked over to my dressing table and saw my jewelry drawer. I carefully went over to it still treading very gingerly picking my way around the rubble on what was left of the now damaged floor. I didn't care though as I was on a mission of hope to see if my jewelry was still there.

I looked to see my jewelry box inside sitting just where I remembered leaving it. My mind was racing, could they still be inside? I carefully opened the box, my heart racing with hope and I held my breath as I opened the box only to see the box was empty and all my jewelry had been stolen. I can't explain the emotions I felt at that precise moment. I just stood there stunned, in shock, not moving. Then I rummaged through the drawer hoping against hope the jewels were somehow still in the drawer, maybe hidden under my other things. Although I knew deep inside, they could not be there, we always have hope. But there was nothing. I looked again in disbelief, picking up my empty jewelry box that just a few days before had contained all the jewelry, I had collected over time. It had all vanished.

Now I cried feeling waves of mixed emotions surging through my entire being, as I stood in my destroyed home. This was a closure I hoped would not happen but there I was standing in the ruins of my home.

I cannot imagine why looters would take the time to search my bedroom, ignore all the very expensive designer clothes, shoes and handbags and have the time to open a drawer, find my jewelry box, steal what they could then close both the box and the drawer. Anyway, I had more serious problems to deal with now, like getting back on my feet and leaving Malibu.

As so many people say after they have been robbed, the invasion of privacy was the worst part, which was the same for me too. Someone had been into our home, gone through my personal things, taken their time, and stolen my jewelry. These items were special to me, and not to mention the pictures that were now gone. This broke my heart.

I know I've said this before but it came to mind daily. *How did the looters manage to get into our neighborhood when the residents weren't even allowed to enter?* This did not make sense.

A better news story would have been to show the police making arrests. If the police were there, we couldn't see them protecting our neighborhood, at least not while the looters were there. So I wondered, *why did the looters have a better plan than the police who were supposed to be protecting our neighborhoods?*

I was not the only person affected, there were many others who also lost their homes and were in the same position as me. Our area was once beautiful and now it would have to be re-built. I don't feel comfortable living there anymore as it lacks resources to support the residents.

The worst thing was the smell of putrid smoke that impregnated every single item. I tried to save my favorite Chanel clutch bag and took it with me to clean it but even a year after it still smelled of smoke, so I threw it away, another thing gone.

There were news videos that showed my neighbors with guns, protecting their homes from these looters that they too had watched the looting as it was happening in our neighborhood. They stood there, in the street as a challenge to any and all of those looters who dared to come into, what was my former neighborhood. They were daring them to come and do their looting!

As I watched what was going on, I could see no police "protecting and serving." This was, for me and others from my small community, being unable to protect our homes, probably the worst of the experience knowing that people we thought were there to protect us did not, in fact, protect or serve us. I mentioned the lack of warning before the fire struck. We were not a huge community and a loudspeaker going around our streets would have helped. This fact came out in the long-awaited Woolsey Fire report. I felt sad that my former neighbors had to take matters into their own hands because our local police were not there!

The following is an excerpt from the final Woolsey Fire Official Report released a year later:

"Emergency management officials were unprepared for massive evacuations before the most destructive fire in Los Angeles County history. It caused chaos through a wind-blown blaze of epic proportions." The report said the Woolsey Fire should serve as a warning when multiple fires break out at once.

"It caused billions in damages and at least three deaths. Officials were critical of the firefight and communication breakdowns, along with a scarcity of air tanker support, equipment, and firefighters. There were no clear warnings to residents about their role in this or future similar emergencies," adding, "The Woolsey Fire forced firefighters to compete for resources as fires other areas had broken out 30 minutes earlier and closer to homes and buildings."

Chapter 27:

Beyond Repair

Things can change in an instant, we have to deal with this fact
— Blanca Blanco

I finally was able to see how much damage had been done, and hopefully, get some closure. When I arrived, I saw that my home was now "Red Signed" which means the structure was a total loss and we were only allowed on our property for a few minutes. I was determined to see for myself how bad the damage was. As you can see from the photos my entire home was destroyed. Worse still, was the choking smell of smoke, which was in everything I looked at.

Now looking through the rubble of what was only a short time before, our beautiful home, there was nothing left of it. Only rubble remained, but I had to see this for myself. This saddened and angered me, making me even more depressed.

I wanted to know what happened and how it happened so I researched to see what I could find. As I was to find out later, the Woolsey Fire was a destructive wildfire that had burned in Los Angeles and Ventura Counties. The fire started on November 8, 2018, and burned 96,949 acres of land, killing three people. It was one of several fires in California that ignited on the same day.

The fire had raced through the chaparral-covered steep canyons with the historic movie and TV sets, small ranches, and the houses of celebrities.

Hundreds of houses in Malibu were destroyed or damaged on both sides of the Pacific Coast Highway. Many of these were on Point Dume where we had lived, that part of Malibu that sticks out from the narrow coastal terrace that lies between the mountains and the Pacific Ocean.

We weren't the only ones who lost our home, other people who lost their homes in Malibu included, our friend Gerard Butler, Miley Cyrus, Robin Thicke, and Shannen Doherty. My heart goes out to them and everyone else who lost their home.

Here is my first look at the remains of our home following the damage done by the fire. The toxic smell of the fire was dangerous to breathe in, causing me to wear a mask.

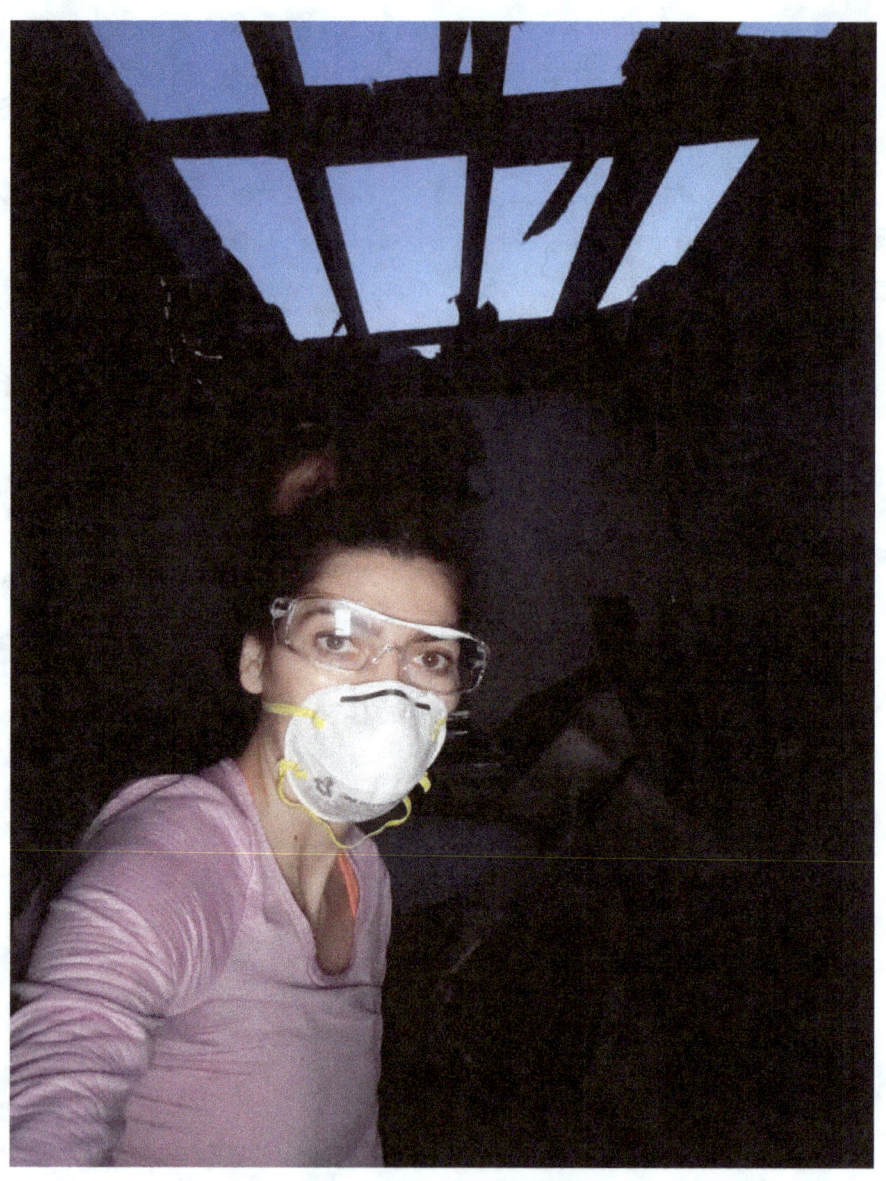

Inside our "unsafe home," the air was filled with choking carcinogens that smelled awful. I had to wear a mask (before COVID-19). Seeing the remnants of our beautiful home was very hard to take in.

Returning to our home, a second time, after the initial assessment. It was as bad as we remembered it. I'm looking at a pile of rubble that was once our beautiful home.

With Star-Star at the restaurant. Very much relieved to have made it through the fire. This photo was taken after we saw our home burn down on TV.

Star-Star at just 4 oz, helped us both get through the fire and helped me focus my thoughts on saving us both.

I found my degree from Washington State University. It had fallen off the wall and had been buried under a heap of rubble which saved it from being too damaged.

Chapter 28:

Getting Back To My Schedule

Are you breathing? Be thankful you are breathing with no pain.
Live for today. — Blanca Blanco

The following week after the fire, one good thing to help me get moving again, and get my strength back, was to follow up with my commitment to attend the Latin Grammys. That event helped me to get out of my "funk" and move again. It's easy to succumb to the sadness, hopelessness, depression, and anger following such a traumatic experience, but taking it one day at a time and being kind to ourselves will make us feel better.

I try not to dwell on the negatives that have happened in my past. Instead, I am a survivor by taking responsibility and ownership of my actions. I believe in processing emotions, but I can tell you all that if we don't allow ourselves to process traumatic events, they can become a big black hole that is always in front of us. I knew I didn't want that to happen. On the contrary, I wanted to face what I was dealing with and be proactive with my actions. I can't change the past but I can certainly change my future. We all have the power within us to do this—*although sometimes we need help.*

Many of my friends and business contacts called me to see if I was ok and to ask if there was anything they could do for me. I appreciated their care and support. It was so sweet of them and they made me feel loved.

Although I was still in shock while doing the press line at the Latin Grammys, I had to put my "game face" on as I wanted to be professional and many of my photographer friends checked in with me too. It was so sweet of them. I really don't remember much about that trip. I was interviewed many times on the Red Carpet and was able to complete all that I had agreed to do successfully despite my underlying anxiety.

As I watched myself on TV doing the interviews, nothing showed on my face at all. I knew I was less than my usual self but I wanted to deliver professional interviews while I was there. One photographer, who knew about the fire, and that it had destroyed my neighborhood, told me how happy he was to see me there.

I didn't engage much in conversations with anyone about the fire. However, sometime later, I found out that one photographer had also lost his home and all his belongings to a fire as well.

On my return, I had a lot of publicity. The many interviews I was asked to do, were now therapeutic for me and helped me talk about my experience, and helped me to move forward past this awful episode faster. I won't downplay how I felt as I was still in shock, but I compartmentalized my feelings to separate what I was doing on the Red Carpet from my trauma.

I worked on finding my inner strength to be able to function, to complete tasks, despite the situation I was in. Once we stop, because of our fear, sadness, or anxiety, then that becomes a concern because the emotional state is dominating our life. We must allow the emotions to be there to process them but also we must take action moving forward to heal and not to hide behind the sheets.

Even though I was feeling anxiety during the Red Carpet event, it helped when I focused on the photographers; engaging and following directions with them. When I was following their directions, they helped keep my mind off the fire. I worked to find my inner strength to finish each section on the Red Carpet successfully, which also helped with my overall healing process. When I saw the digital images, I was proud of myself for following through with my commitments.

Chapter 29:

Dealing With Loss

Dealing with loss is a sad part of life. It's how we deal with it that separates us all. – Blanca Blanco

I now had to face dealing with the loss. But I have to say it wasn't just losing my home and all my things, it was also my inability to have any control of what had gone on during that awful drive through the fire. Then seeing my home being destroyed on the TV news in the restaurant and seeing the looting in my neighborhood being filmed, but apparently, not being stopped. The theft and destruction of all I had owned, then finally not being allowed to go back while looting was going on, left me feeling helpless and very angry!

Our emotions are interconnected and during a trauma like this, other feelings from childhood or other highly stressful periods in our life all seem to highlight and reactivate those emotions as well.

In a way, blocking some childhood traumas was a defense mechanism for me in order to be able to function on a day-to-day basis. I am aware sometimes traumatic experiences can lead people to addiction. I am very grateful my siblings and I, despite our situation, became successful and productive members of society and we took responsibility for our actions. Having our mother as a strong source of support also gave us the strength to become who we are today. One thing we used to do at night was to lay in bed and talk to each other about our day and often we would laugh so hard seeing the funny side of our day's stories. Another thing was that mom always brushed my hair and made braids, which was very relaxing for me.

From my education, focused on psychology and social work, I understood that one day these events, in my childhood, would eventually resurface and have to be dealt with. As a child, I thought I could deal with these things behind a closed door in my mind. There was a sense of shame and we just wanted to be looked at like a normal family. But what defines normal, right? As I got older, I learned to address those emotions, which led to strengthening who I am and in turn, led to my personal growth.

I am grateful to be alive and that the fire only took my material things, but the reality was still there, with me dealing with deep sadness and my feelings of hopelessness. I had to work every day so I used positive "self-talk" to be able to process all that had happened, to move forward, and not get overwhelmed. I realized that others had lost more than I did. But this is not about comparisons, it is about managing the very personal feelings of deep sadness and hopelessness. I now felt that in understanding this, I would be able to begin to work it through.

Abuse and trauma affect us in many areas of our lives. For example, our sense of self, self-esteem, and self-efficacy are negatively impacted. However, it's important to know that after experiencing a traumatic event research shows that one is more likely to experience Post Traumatic Growth by 66% than PTSD 25%. Post Traumatic Growth can be life-changing because it allows us to create positive psychological changes in our lives. Giving us new direction and guidance. As we work towards healing our past traumas, we learn how more resilient we are, and that gives us more courage, determination, and adaptability. Without the trauma, we wouldn't have known to what degree we are capable of overcoming. And to know that growth happens as a direct result of traumas can help us look at the situation from a more positive perspective.

We all have to deal with loss at some point in our lives, whether it be the loss of a family member, or a close friend, a divorce, or something else. Our lives are not linear so we will experience a range of emotions because of that. These are the facts of life, but they don't have to become anything long-term. Learning techniques and getting help is a phone call away and I'm not talking about expensive therapy since there are many free helplines available with dedicated people who are there to offer guidance to get you through.

I would like to add some tips that have worked for me especially when dealing with my anxiety and mild depression after the Woolsey fire. This is what I learned from the trauma and how it affected me.

Don't isolate yourself: Stay in touch with people because once we withdraw the sadness worsens. I know, however, that talking hurts when we have depression, from heavy emotional pain. But taking baby steps, like sending a text, or creating a WhatsApp group, calling family members, or a friend, and sharing how we are feeling will help our mood and make us feel better. Have a group of friends to be part of your "lifeline" who you know you can reach when you are feeling down. I often used WhatsApp to call my group of family and friends and checked in with them especially when I was dealing with anxiety. I felt better knowing someone was aware of what was going on and who could check in with me.

Stay Active and Gain Endorphins: Even though our energy during anxiety and depression is very low, even just taking a walk will help us feel better because it has been proved that exercise helps our mental health and our mood. The reason for that is when we exercise our body releases a chemical called endorphins that trigger positive feelings. I know I would at least try to walk around my block, check the mailbox and feel the air. That was a challenging task to do, as I would have preferred to stay at home but I felt better afterward.

Face Your Fears: Acknowledging that we are dealing with anxiety and depression is a major step to recovery. Avoidance is not going to help with the situation instead it will just keep adding to the depression because we are not addressing the issue. Embrace your anxiety and know you are both working together to manage life. I named my anxiety and made it a new "friend" in my life.

In my case, I wanted to avoid doing things that triggered my anxiety, but instead, I had to learn to confront my fears. Our triggers make us feel like we are in danger or something tragic is going to happen. I had to learn to break the negative pattern associated with my fear. When that happens, we are unable to control our reactions. Working with a therapist and doing exposure therapy helped me to overcome the fear of flying. I couldn't avoid flying so instead I faced the fears of flying head-on.

Now I can fly alone with no problems. The reason is that I exposed myself to that fear in a "safe" place, like with my therapist. I worked at unlearning negative associations and with practice, I decreased the reaction to the fear. I only had one panic attack during flying but the fear of it happening again was lingering in the back of my mind. A big part of my career was to fly to many places for work, and I would not allow that fear to control all areas of my life. It is a stressful process when one is facing their fears, but the tools I used helped me to broaden my experience instead of limiting it. Additionally, I'm proud to say in the last ten years I have overcome the fear of flying. It took lots of hard work, determination, and daily use of the "tools" which helped me overcome my fear. It also gave me a burst of confidence that motivated me because I knew I had achieved a goal.

Create a Toolbox: This is not a toolbox for hammers and screwdrivers, it is for storing tools and techniques, that you know will work for you when you are experiencing anxiety or depression. For example, when I flew, I would bring my favorite pink blanket. I would draw, listen to music, type on my laptop, wear my flying soft socks, use lavender oil, and do some journaling. I had to use so many tools to overcome this fear of flying because no matter what, flying is part of my career and I had to overcome it. It's a choice I made. Focusing on a task is helpful because it is a distraction and we focus less on the anxiety.

Healthy Choices: Make sure you don't skip meals because that helps regulate your sugar levels. Stay away from recreational drugs and excessive use of alcohol. Remember to do your yearly physical because blood work will show if you have an underlying health condition. For example, anxiety and depression can be triggered by hypothyroidism.

Seek Help: There is no shame in seeking help. At some point in our lives, all of us will probably need to seek help or receive therapy. There is no shame in this, we are not perfect and sometimes we just need some guidance and tools to keep our minds more organized.

Have a Routine: Having a daily "to-do" list helps even if you are just alone at home. When I was at my lowest point my "to do" list was to shower, brush my hair, eat breakfast, call mom, organize one drawer in my room.

"Love" Post-it Notes: I ordered bright, colorful "Post-It" pads from Amazon and wrote positive affirmations, like, "I am strong!" "You can do it!" "You are a diamond!" and other positive messages. Then I placed them in areas of my house or in my car. Then, when I walked by, I would read them and take that message in. Taking this step helps us (don't read and drive), but before you start driving check in with your "Post-It", then repeat it in your head over and over. This helps so much.

Chapter 30:

Positive Self-Talk

It is during our darkest moments that we must focus to see the light. — Aristotle

Our self-talk can be quite critical. We are constantly judging and being hard on ourselves. It is a learned behavior that starts in childhood. As a child, for example in school, we are conditioned to reward winning and not lose during sports. As a society, we are conditioned to believe only in a reward based on good results. So this creates a narrow, "black and white" mentality, meaning an all-or-nothing kind of thinking. Creating unrealistic expectations can lead to a cycle of guilt and negative self-talk.

I know I'm guilty of that, but on a regular basis, I check in with myself and try to work on being kinder to myself. Negative self-talk will hinder our learning and often our progress. Changing the negative to positive self-talk (positive thinking) helps us understand our thinking pattern and help us to challenge it. Of course, we may not always change the situation, or the issue that caused it, but one thing we can do is try to shift our perspectives.

I utilized "re-framing" often even as a child but I didn't realize I was doing it. According to the American Psychological Association, Re-framing is a process of re-conceptualizing a problem by seeing it from a different perspective. I had to shift my perspective to positive self-talk and take a positive stand on the situation. This allows any of us to recognize the issue and make a positive stand in each situation. I had to accept that I could not change the past but I can control, by taking action, the future to create a positive solution. At the end of the chapter, I share some Re-framing Positive Talk examples that I have been able to apply to my life and it definitely helped me when I found myself re-thinking about the fire over and over again. I had to shift my perspective to positive self-talk. I accepted that I could not change the past but I could manage, by taking action, for the future.

For example, when these dark thoughts came back, often in waves and at night while I was sleeping, I would just stop what I was doing, pause myself, take some deep breaths, shift my thinking instead from "Why did this happen to me?" to say, "What did it teach me?" Or from "I lost everything." I would say "I gained personal growth and experience." I also re-framed to "I am alive and I can re-gain most of what I lost." By doing this, we can all work on what we lost and deal with the result more positively.

But sometimes this can lead to the "what ifs." W*hat if* we didn't get away from the house. *What if* we couldn't save Star-Star, or *what if* I was unable to wake John, or *what if* we got stuck on the PCH with the fire coming in hot and fast. I realized these were natural fears, but I also knew I would not go down that rabbit hole (sorry Star-Star) of negativity. I can't change the outcome of what just happened and these thoughts always lead nowhere. This is negative thinking and this would never do if I was to get through all that had happened.

Other more positive thoughts I used, were looking for and finding a new home and where we would live next. These were positive thoughts for me as I could imagine what our next home might look like. Taking forward action activates the sense of hope for the future and I was very busy dealing with the insurance company and the many other things I had to take care of "now" in order to take the necessary steps forward. It was time-consuming but the insurance company I was dealing with was very sympathetic and their staff helped me to start thinking of solutions. "Action Thinking" helps us face the worry of the situation we have faced and therefore helps us to take steps to move forward.

I focused, most of all, on getting back to work as that was my passion. I had hundreds of well-wishers, from my business dealings, and friends, sending me messages of love and positive vibes. These messages really lifted me up more than they probably realized. I often used to sit on the bed, in our temporary hotel room and go through them. I always felt better after reading their messages of love. As I mentioned before, positive affirmations are so important and this makes our days go a lot smoother. Having a non-toxic circle of friends also makes a big difference.

Part of re-framing is to know in advance when we are going down the path of negative thoughts that seem never-ending and are often random. The reality is that we will always have these negative thoughts, so learning how to manage them, nourish them and create positive patterns that we are most comfortable with, will make our lives much easier.

I knew I had to switch from these thoughts and focus on what made me happy. Fortunately, I had many things do this for me; writing my book, being on set, traveling, hanging out with family and friends, even chatting on the phone. I would literally, "shift" from the negatives and focus on positives.

I love watching comedy shows which are very therapeutic for me. We are all able to do this and label it, "re-framing" our thoughts or "positive thinking." This sets us up for a different train of thought and begins the process of getting out of the "hole" we are in.

I loved listening to comedians on YouTube or TV. This always made me happy. One person I can tell you about was Jimmy Kimmel's sidekick, Guillermo Rodriguez. I would watch the Jimmy Kimmel show and Guillermo made me laugh so much even thinking about some of his stunts on Jimmy Kimmel's show helped to break my mood and re-frame my mind.

He had interviewed me on the Red Carpet at the Oscars several years in a row. One time he offered me a sip of tequila (I'm not a tequila girl and I don't drink on the job) but it was so funny. Our interviews were partly in Spanglish, meaning Spanish and English, which were hilarious to see. In another interview, he had some Cheetos with him. Those chips leave your mouth and fingers bright orange if you touch them! We did eventually eat one together, laughing the entire time.

My point here is to show how when we are experiencing intrusive thoughts, pause and re-frame them into constructive, positive thoughts. Something funny, or sweet, or just a great time we once had will work to lift our spirits back up. I enjoy watching videos about bunnies they make my heart happy and bring me so much joy, so I tend to do that often. Remember, you cannot direct the winds but you can adjust your hair!

One cannot ignore that anxiety and depression are big issues, but we can use tools to try to manage day-to-day life. Addressing it is a healthy way to help us resolve many issues from becoming an obstacle in the future. Our brains are incredible and will always do what needs to be done to help protect us. Remember, recognizing being vulnerable takes great courage and it's okay to say I am not okay, take a pause, and start again.

We can never change the past, but we can make changes that affect the future. We should try to make life as positive as possible and we can do this by re-framing. It will also help from becoming anxious, upset, and angry, to becoming more hopeful, optimistic, motivated, and in control.

We all have to make decisions and making it a positive or negative experience is our choice, so select a positive experience, which tends to be easier on ourselves, mentally and physically. We own that control!

Re-Framing and Positive Self-Talk:

I used the following techniques to help me:

INSTEAD OF THIS	TRY THIS
I can't do this.	I can try. I am allowed to make mistakes.
I have so many barriers.	Great opportunity to challenge myself.
Why do I need to wear a mask?	I'm a hero, saving other people's lives.
I was anxious at the meeting.	I successfully completed it despite feeling anxious
Why did this happen to me?	What did this teach me?
I cried so much; I made a fool of myself.	Being vulnerable takes courage.
I feel I'm losing control.	These thoughts don't define me.
I suck.	I'm a work in progress.

INSTEAD OF THIS	TRY THIS
With the pandemic, my life is so boring.	Now I can focus on myself.
I can't get through this.	I'm strong and resilient.
I'm such a failure	I'm learning and gaining experience.

Chapter 31:

Getting Back on the Horse

Adversity is neither friend nor foe. It is a common acquaintance whose presence is least desired, but most rewarding when embraced. — Carolyn Wells

Now I use the tools to get on with my life and take steps to move forward. Working was the best way forward.

Two weeks after we lost our home in Malibu, I had to fly to Marrakesh to the attend Marrakesh Film Festival and I also had scheduled Grazia and HOLA magazine editorials and interviews. Upon arriving at Murano Resort in Marrakesh, they had so many flowers for me including red rose petals in the bed, in the walkway, and a beautiful bouquet of fruit in my room. The cutest thing, which I had never seen before was that they even scattered rose petals inside the toilet!

I will always be grateful for the warm welcome. They even had fresh mint tea for me and had my 2-hour massage ready when I wanted it. I believe my French designer and good friend, Christophe Guillarme, had a lot to do with letting them know what I had been going through and the Murano resort wanted to provide a safe and pleasant welcome. Another amazing thing was that they had brought a camel into the hotel so I could do some amazing photoshoots. I had never seen a camel in person so it was so sweet of them. The camel was beautiful!

As I stepped into the press line, the first night at the festival several media outlets were making sweet stories about my look on the Marrakesh Red Carpet and how I had been visiting specific areas of the beautiful city. To my media friends, you know who you are, I will be forever full of gratitude for what you did during that difficult time in my life. I thank you for your continued support with fabulous stories and your friendship.

Looking at their stories made me smile because just 2 weeks before that I was fighting the battle of my life trying to keep calm and to manage an anxiety attack while driving through the Woolsey Fire. Now the great headlines about my trip to Marrakesh were so cool and even better when they mentioned, the film I was part of, *Hold On,* that hit theaters during that time.

We all have to heal and it is different for all of us. Simply repressing feelings, which cause us pain, is not healthy. But feeling and seeing things in a positive frame of mind is part of the healing process. Healing takes time. It is normal to experience as a reaction to a loss. Although I was dealing with loss, I was feeling a sense of gratitude for knowing I was alive and healthy after that experience.

One thing for certain, we cannot change the past, but we can change how we deal with the situation and how we choose to continue to live our lives. Many friends tell me of problems they had in their past, still have difficulties letting go. As a result, this affects their present life. I would say to my friends, that we all have to accept that the past cannot be changed now. We cannot go back to "yesterday" however you can change the present. You

194

can take your past experiences and learn from them, by applying them to the present and the personal growth gained from the past will help to manage and take proper action for the future.

I know for me, the smell of smoke triggered the traumatic memories of the Woolsey fire. I became aware of that and worked on knowing that I would be okay. It's normal to make that association because it was such a traumatic experience. I knew eventually I would overcome it.

The alternative becomes a big black hole we tiptoe around that is triggered every time a word, an image, a sound, or even a smell occurs. Then we are right back in that negative world inside our mind. We can all overcome these challenges, it takes time and sometimes we need professional help. For me with all I knew and all I had been trained to understand, my way of "getting back on the horse," was to get right back into work as my way of dealing with what happened. We cannot ever change the past, but as I am showing here, we can change how we deal with, and try to manage, our future.

Sharing What I Learned That Worked For Me

1. Taking baby steps after a traumatic experience is the key.

2. Be aware that emotions are temporary and there is light at end of the tunnel.

3. Sometimes taking a day off is a way of healing and taking care of YOU.

4. After you fall, the good news uphill is next. Life is about balance.

5. Emotional pain and physical pain are normal processes of grieving.

Laugh and the World Laughs With You

Many have heard the words, *"Laugh and the world laughs with you, cry and you cry alone."* These beautiful words are from a poem, *"Solitude,"* written by Ella Wheeler Wilcox. Her beautiful words explain this perfectly. I love this poem and thought I would share it with you.

"Solitude," by Ella Wheeler Wilcox
courtesy of *The Poetry Foundation*

Laugh and the world laughs with you
Weep and you weep alone
For the sad old earth must borrow its mirth,
But has trouble enough of its own.

Sing and the hills will answer
Sigh, it is lost on the air
The echoes bound to a joyful sound,
But shrink from voicing care.

Rejoice and men will seek you
Grieve and they turn and go
They want full measure of all your pleasure,
But they do not need your woe.

Be glad and your friends are many
Be sad and you lose them all, —
There are none to decline your nectared wine,
But alone you must drink life's gall.

Feast and your halls are crowded,
Fast and the world goes by.
Succeed and give and it helps you live,

But no man can help you die.

There is room in the halls of pleasure
For a large and lordly train,
But one by one we must all file on
Through the narrow aisles of pain.

How true these beautiful words are and, to me, they describe perfectly the emotions we all feel from time to time. We each must weave a new success for ourselves whatever this is for each of us because one thing is for certain if we don't decide to, we will never have the fulfilling life we could have. In her poem, Ella is saying we all have to move on in order to have a fulfilling life and in moving on we can reach our success. I strongly believe expressing vulnerability takes so much courage, and deciding to take steps forward speaks volumes.

Chapter 32:

Life is Short

*Many never have the time to prepare to lose a loved one. —
Blanca Blanco*

I want to explain how important our mom was in our lives.

It was June 2021, when I received an urgent call from my brother, from Washington State, saying mom was in the hospital and she was in her last days. He didn't have any other information until the doctors returned after doing their rounds.

That call turned my life upside down. All the excitement and hope I was experiencing, just before that call, had just vanished in a second. I only remember parts of the call — *I have something to tell you, she is in her last days, there is not much we can do.*

My thoughts and emotions were all over the place. I was in full panic mode. What is life without mom? She is so young at only 62, how did it happen so quickly? A sense of guilt was there too because at that exact moment I was not with her. Although when I spoke with mom, she was in good spirits. That made me even sadder to believe she is protecting me from the truth.

I couldn't stop pacing back and forth in my hotel room and after that call I called my sister, asking her to explain to me what she had heard, because I only remembered certain parts of the call. I had dropped everything and caught a flight up to Washington then made my way as fast as I could to see her. I was hoping nothing would happen before I got there. When I received the call, I was in Atlanta working, staying in a hotel, doing laundry, and ended up flying with my wet clothes, in my suitcase. Definitely, for me, that was a first!

From the moment I got the call to my journey to the airport, time felt surreal. My mind and my emotions were somewhere else but my body was on the way to the airport. The disconnection was prevalent. I haven't experienced anxiety for quite a while and this news definitely reactivated it. I was still in full panic mode. I messaged my lifeline group of friends on WhatsApp to let them know the situation and to ensure they would be on standby If I needed to talk. My friends and my sisters were all there for me via phone or WhatsApp if I needed their emotional support.

That flight was the longest and saddest flight I have ever experienced. I cried most for most of the flight. It was not a regular crying. It was filled with deep, gut-wrenching sobs that I couldn't stop while on the plane. I even laid down as I was the only one in the row. I could see my chest and stomach rising hard and fast. My eyes were swollen from crying and I am certain other flyers saw me and heard me. During the flight, I was able to get Wi-Fi so I messaged my WhatsApp group to share how I was feeling.

We are not born with instructions on how to deal or manage with losing a parent, a sibling, or a child. It's the deepest pain in the world and even though mom was still alive, I knew what was coming. I wanted to stop time or pause it and wished I could go back so I could have spent more time with her. The guilt was there, big time, but I had to add positive self-talk. I reminded myself to take steps during this process. I took deep breaths and reminded myself, I am not alone,

I have my siblings and together we will be going through the changes and we will support each other.

I permitted myself to cry as I knew I didn't want to repress what I was now feeling and after each time I cried, I felt a little better. I did focus on how I would be okay, and how I wanted to be there for mom.

After arriving at Spokane, Washington, I went straight to the hospital. She was indeed very sick and having worked with hospice care I knew how serious this was for her.

After talking with the hospital staff, I fully understood that her heart attack caused considerable damage and this was not reversible. She had heart failure and also had renal failure. Sadly, my mom would not survive this latest episode. It was shocking to me. She was always full of energy and even now, she didn't even look sick. She had a heart attack 10 years ago and had been going to her cardiac checkups, eventually, she only went in for regular check-ups, from her primary care doctor. Things have now gone downhill — *very quickly*.

Now all of the sudden, we are told by her cardiologist and kidney doctor that there is no hope. There was nothing in our control that any of us could do. It felt very hopeless. I continued to advocate tirelessly for my mom to find a solution with her medical team but the only solution we had was to provide hospice care.

Really? There is nothing else we can do? I felt numb, empty, and heartbroken. We know these types of situations are going to happen in our lives one day, but we really don't think it's going to happen to us that fast. This was a reality for me now and I will soon be joining that part of the population that will not have a parent, my Mami, my foundation, the glue in my family will not be there for me or any of us anymore. To never hear her contagious laugh and see her beautiful smile brought me again to tears. Not ever being able to do our video chats on WhatsApp, or to call her when I am packing, or to call her when something funny happened.

These thoughts gave me shivers and tears and I wished I had more time with her. I wished we could pause time. The deep pain in my stomach was there and it felt like a dream that I wanted to wake up from.

After she was given her terminal diagnosis, she felt that one of her doctors treated her as though she was a burden or lost cause. We resolved the situation but I want to remind anyone or any doctor when someone is diagnosed terminally they are still alive, they are only dying when they take their last breath. So treat them with kindness, respect, and dignity.

The one thing I could do is sit with my mom in the hospital and hold her hand, brush and braid her hair, as she used to do for me, and share some moments we had experienced together. It is okay at times, to just be there, sitting in silence. I would see her eyes, full of life, history, and curiosity looking at me. I could also see her inner strength was still strong although her body was becoming weaker.

Seeing her now so vulnerable, lying in bed, brought in a deep sense of sadness because mom was always on the go and was such an independent person. Now seeing her in this hospital bed, using a walker, so fragile, I knew it made her uncomfortable but she didn't show it. I never visualized my life without my mom, we never do. I know this sounds crazy but I always hoped she would be with me forever physically and I never imagined her not being there for us. So, please hug your mom and don't assume any of our moms are here forever because life does not work like that, and it sucks!

At the hospital as I sat, just to be there with mom, holding her hand for hours, filling her with loving memories, telling her how much I loved her. This was my priority now. But also, mom needed help with the next steps so I had to work on that too, things like hospice and care for her at home. Since I had experience with hospice, I took on that role.

While we were at the hospital mom asked me to take care of a few things for her before she leaves this physical world and so I, together with my siblings, worked on that with her. We definitely worked well as a team, despite a few personality differences but our anxiety got to all of us. At my hotel room in the night (while mom was in the hospital), we were all trying to sleep but we were crying, bawling, and trying to fall asleep. There was nothing that could have changed the prognosis and we just had to face everything that was happening around us. Crying was therapeutic and we needed it to process our emotions.

Mom was the glue that held our family together. She defended us against our sometimes aggressive father keeping us all safe, deflecting his many rants aimed at us and her. Mom had a larger-than-life personality, but dad often insulted her size and her demeanor right in front of us, trying to belittle her. We would always jump to her defense because when he did this it hurt her feelings, making her sad. She always just let these things go to keep the peace at home, but we could tell that his words would chip away at her spirit. Growing up, we encouraged mom to separate from dad but she wanted to keep the family unit together, as that was so important to her, since she grew up with only one parent and knew what that would be like for us.

Mom was the life and soul of our family, she always kept a cheerful outlook, laughing and singing to us when we were kids and we loved her very much. Without her, there would have been no family. She was naturally funny, doing funny things to make us laugh, whenever we were down, she would lift us up.

She always made things better and remained, at least to us, happy and would never allow her surroundings to bring her down. She cared for dad when his hands were so sore from the hard work he had to do. While we were all at school, she kept busy looking after the orchard workers' kids as their babysitter.

As sick as she was, she warned us about dad's manipulating behavior and told us to be careful and not to allow him to insult any of us. She made a point to each of us to never allow distance to separate us all. She knew she was not going to survive much longer. We were now all together, just there happy to be in her company.

This stress began to create an imbalance within our family. Disagreements, discontent, and so on, because everyone's emotions were running high and all of us were on edge daily not knowing if each day would be our Mami's last. Everyone was exhausted, and difficult decisions, now needed to be made on a daily basis. Despite a few differences, we did have one strong commonality, to fill our mom's remaining time with loving memories.

Our Mami gave so much of her heart to everyone she came in contact with. She was an honest and loyal friend. She was there for people in the good and bad times.

I believe her calmness was the result of her being guided. My mom's bravery and strength were beautiful to witness despite the horrible situation.

I remember the morning before she passed, I was seated next to her, gently holding her hand and just looking at her, when she suddenly opened her eyes and the first thing she said was just one word, "Mami" she was looking past me, so I would love to think my sweet grandma was there preparing her for her journey. When she said "Mami" it was not a question, it was like a statement like mom you are here. It gave me a sense of peace to see she had that heavenly support. A journey which she knew had to face alone when detaching from the physical world to the "unknown" world, but to know she had grandma, her own Mami present with her, made me happy. It was a bittersweet moment.

I wanted to walk her to the other side and see what she saw to make sure she would be okay. Of course, reality does not work like that. But that thought crossed my mind and I wished I knew what grandma told her. How was grandma doing? It all gave us a sense of sadness but we were also happy to know she was not alone they would be together soon. This is a testament to the closeness my mother and grandmother had, so close that even though my siblings and I were there, we were not able to go through the exit journey with her. She had my grandma to guide her and protect her. She was not on any painkillers at the time, she said what she said.

The hardest thing for me was to see her illness progress and see her decline as things got worse for her. She was always independent and seeing her bedridden was so hard for us to watch.

I remember the day before mom passed, we were helping her use the commode, her legs were so weak and she couldn't move them anymore. She looked at me and said, my legs are giving up, I am getting worse. This was the first and only time I saw the fear, sadness, and defeated look in her eyes. This made us all so very sad. We did all we could do and I told her, "I am here for you. You are so brave, mom, and you are not alone."

At the hospital, doctors encouraged mom to eat anything she desired because her health outcome would not change. Even then, mom only wanted to eat healthy stuff and was hopeful it would make a difference. Mom at the end of her life had an adverse reaction to foods that were not healthy.

Despite everything, we got through those tough times because we are a close family.

A Sudden Awakening

As I said, we all dropped what we were doing and went to our mother to care for her to make sure she was comfortable, loved and we wanted to make all her wishes come true. We did, and I can tell you she was so happy to have us all around her at this time in her life. My mom's sisters from California also drove long hours to come to Washington, to see and care for her too. Mom was loved by many people with who she came in contact.

I spent about a month with mom at home helping her in whatever way I could and took on many roles as her caregiver, providing emotional support, housekeeping, cooking, driving, and pretty much anything I could do to ensure she was comfortable and felt loved. All my siblings, bless their hearts, were there also providing their support. Every one of us helped in a different capacity to care for my mom. We each took on our different roles that were best suited for mom's care.

"Caregiver burnout" is real, and I know we each experienced it at one point or another while taking care of mom. My brother prayed for hours with mom daily as mom looked on proudly with a sense of comfort. He would set the iPad to play soothing music. I saw how unhelpful my father could be, he would occasionally help with her but at times he would still say hurtful things to mom. I have been very respectful towards him for years despite his bad behavior, but this was enough.

When we asked him to please refrain from being mean to mom and to instead apologize to her, he in return, got up and tried to push me, I was near mom's bed (she had gone to the bathroom), but I knew she had heard the commotion. My siblings were telling dad to stop and they took me out of the living room. He did not believe he needed to apologize to mom for all the mistreatment over the years. Instead, he thought she should apologize to him! I was very disappointed but not surprised at his reaction. I had enough of his attitude and would not allow him to mistreat any of us ever again.

I told him that this is the last stage for mom and to find it in his heart to be extra nice, or at least pretend to be nice, for her sake. He became angry and told me he is my dad and I needed to respect him. I was so upset with him I told him respect is something you need to earn.

I finally stood up to him. It surprised him to see how strong I had become. I was not at all scared of him now and I would never be intimidated by him ever again.

I'm not here to justify his behavior, but no longer will I keep it behind doors, out of respect and shame. I know a few family members will be angry but it's my experience, I lived it. It's my story and I am taking ownership.

My mom's lifelong friend, who has known my mother for over 40 years, was there for her during the good and bad times, and now with her at the end of her life, wanted to know if dad had asked for forgiveness from mom. Mom's dear friend had witnessed over all these years the continuous mistreatment and abuse she had received from our dad. She was disappointed when she learned dad would not take her declining health seriously and apologize.

Mami's health was now declining more and more each day as her ability to move her legs or get up from her bed had become impossible for her. I understood all of what was happening as I had seen it many times. Death was approaching her and we could only help her transition peacefully and keeping everything as positive as we all could. A day before my mom passed away, she asked my two sisters and me to give her a sponge bath in bed. We did that and put her in fresh pajamas, we had tears in our eyes because we knew she was now preparing to approach the end of her life physically, but we also knew mom will be with us spiritually forever.

I have prepared my siblings for the inevitable but it doesn't make it any easier for them or me. We were all treading on eggshells trying to deal with this. We were all super stressed but at the same time, we all had a sense of comfort knowing we were all with mom and helping her to be comfortable. I remember sleeping in the night on her couch next to her hospital bed and although I tried to sleep, I kept waking up at hearing any sound, and the first thing I did was to look to make sure she was still breathing. Even when I was dreaming, I would be doing this.

We are never fully prepared for what we know will happen when we each reach the end of our inevitable journey. It's part of human nature to think of the inevitable as maybe just a possibility with other options available to us if we pray hard. This is what one of my brothers was hoping and praying for, a miracle, which would make her well again. He was the type of kind, hopeful, spiritual person, who believed mom would be cured.

We all understood we were soon to lose our most important family member, our beloved Mami and we were all happy to show her all the love we all felt for her and we wanted her to know we would all be ok after she had gone.

After the hospital, mom was discharged under hospice care to return home. As we walked into her room, she asked us to organize all her jewelry as she would be picking out jewelry items she wanted us each to keep (my mom loved jewelry). At home, we all gathered around her bed while she is giving each of us her jewelry, her goodbye gifts. She had so many things I had given her throughout the years, it was a bittersweet moment when she returned them to me. We would all take turns to go in the kitchen if we wanted to cry, since mom was so happy, smiling and sharing her stories with each specific piece of jewelry.

We all gathered around her bed and we sang with her. It was a very touching moment for us and brought back such happy memories. Mom was laughing, making jokes, and being her normal self, it was beautiful to see her joy. I know her joy was for us, but deep down I was heartbroken. My heart was shattered into pieces and I had to escape to the kitchen many times to cry because I knew these will be our last memories with our beloved Mami. Our thoughts will always warm us when we think of her and we know no matter what, she will remain with us forever in our hearts.

I managed to read a few of the stories to her, from this book as it was still being written, and she was filling in many details. She talked about the celebrations we had when she cooked Mexican dishes for us all. She was in a happy place talking with us and having us there with her, listening to her memories. Amazingly Mami still had her bubbly personality and seemed so happy to contribute her thoughts to my book and it meant so much to add her memories to mine.

She still laughed a lot despite what she knew was happening to her. She remembered also when she was pregnant, we accompanied her to her doctor's appointment. She was very thirsty and needed a drink of water. At this time, we had no money at all. We stepped into a restaurant and asked for some water for her, but they refused! They told us, "If you don't have a quarter, then we can't give you any water!" We told them our mom was pregnant and needed a drink, but it made no difference to them they still refused her. The restaurant is still there in Washington and hopefully, the owners have changed. But Mami wanted me to put this in my book.

Though we will miss her so much, I will always remember her big, beautiful smile, her giggles, her warmth, her caring side and her love to me, and how much she cared and loved my sweet Star-Star bunny. We will remember all the funny things she did and the laughter she brought us. We love you, mom and we'll miss you terribly. Thanks for all the love you showed us and your strength in leading us through all life's lessons we were to face, as a family!

I was happy we were able to organize mom's last birthday party and over 50 family members from all over USA and Mexico visited to celebrate with her and it made her so happy. Everyone that arrived was COVID-19 vaccinated or COVID tested and had to wear a mask around mom, as per the doctor's orders. Mom had also ordered our Christmas gifts and gave them to us since she knew she would not be able to spend Christmas with us. It was a bittersweet time but we celebrated Christmas in June with her. Her happiness to see all of us open our last gifts from her will always stay in my heart. Her biggest joy was when her grandchildren would open the gifts and the laughter and smiles that brought to her.

I wanted to add the things that helped me to get through this most difficult time, so below are, some "tips" that helped me cope during our family's stressful time:

1. Accept and process your emotions.
2. Family dynamics change and that is a normal process.
3. Self-care is essential to avoid burnout.
4. Create goals as a family for the day.
5. Unresolved issues come to the surface, don't ignore them, address them.
6. Deep breathing exercises daily help with anxiety.
7. Take it one day at a time.
8. We cannot pause time. One cannot stop the inevitable from happening. Live for today.

Chapter 33:

In Loving Memory

Spread love everywhere you go. Let no one ever come to you without leaving happier. — Mother Teresa

Our beloved Mami passed away on Friday 18th June 2021, at 7:45 pm. I was holding her hand as she peacefully passed away from this world. She was at peace and fully aware of everything as she passed because she knew she had done all she could to prepare each of us to achieve our dreams. In the words above, from Mother Teresa, she was leaving us all in a far happier place than when we entered into this life.

I want to focus here on all you did for us, Mami. You were taken away from us too soon. Holding your hand as you were passing peacefully was so hard to witness but I will forever be grateful we had the chance to say goodbye. Not everyone gets that privilege.

Seeing your last breath, your last glance, your last smile, laughter, your sweet words is something we were not prepared to let go of. I know your body, mind, and heart were ready to go, but we were not ready to see you go. You were loved by many and impacted many peoples' lives. 💔

Mami took the diagnosis, that her heart had suffered severe damage, with dignity and she faced that journey with so much bravery, inner strength, and with no fear. Her determination to show us not to be afraid and to turn that situation into a learning experience, which she did with a smile that I will remember forever.

We showered her with so many loving memories, we had good days and bad days as her condition progressed; seeing her body decline, becoming so vulnerable was the hardest for us to see since she was always on the go and independent. Helping mom fulfill her wishes before leaving this physical world gave me a sense of purpose and a sad but sweet happiness to see that she completed her checklist. My siblings and I will keep her legacy going and keep the strong sibling bond just as mom raised us to and always wanted us to maintain. She was the glue to the family and her spirit will remain forever to be in our hearts.

There are no instructions on how to deal with our losses and each person" experience is different. I still dial her number, video time her on WhatsApp, wanting to share an experience with her, then I remember she is not here physically. That is the hardest for me to accept and it hurts deeply. We will have good and bad days but remembering Mami's strength will guide my siblings and me throughout our lives.

If not for her strength I would not have been able to succeed in school in the way I did, nor would my brothers and sisters have succeeded either. This was exactly why she wanted us to live the American dream and we thank her for her vision that enabled it to be so.

When I wanted to go to college then to university, Mami supported my applications for scholarships. It was because of her tireless support, that I was able to achieve everything I wanted for my future.

Mami helped all of us succeed in school and helped us focus on getting good grades. We all saw how hard she worked to bring in what little money she could and when Christmas or birthdays occurred, she was the one who made these days special for us; baking a birthday cake, singing songs, and doing goofy things that made us all laugh. These are now treasured memories we will keep with us forever.

Mami was the heart and soul of our family and because of her, we each have some of her drive and fun-loving character. She was strong and when she put her foot down to keep dad in check, he knew not to cross her. The same applied to each of us, when she told us the way it was to be, we did as she said.

Her strength came through when we were all living in those atrocious conditions in the garage, she kept us all positive and made it possible for us as young children to deal with it and not to focus on how bad things were. She was the warmth we had inside us all through those frigid winter months. She showed her positive attitude when teachers from school came to bring us clothes and blankets to help keep us warm.

I am who I am because of my beautiful Mami. My siblings each went to college and, like me, succeeded in getting their degrees.

Mami drove me and supported me to achieve all I could and so far, I have honored her wishes. We will as a family continue to *break the mold* and rise above.

It was our mother who understood this and made it possible for us to succeed and because of her, we are succeeding. She managed the work of babysitting for 12 hours each day, looking after us all, keeping us positive, cooking, and doing all that we needed to live a normal life despite all that life threw at us with the appalling conditions we were living in. When we were sad, she lifted us up with her humor and her singing.

I will make certain that her legacy will continue within me and my siblings. When I asked her if she was afraid Mami said "No tengo miedo" (I am not afraid) as she transitioned peacefully.

Thanks, Mami for all you did, you were an awesome teacher in all you taught us, so rest in peace! We will love you till the end of time.

Mami and me, taken at her home after
her heart attack. A treasured photo.

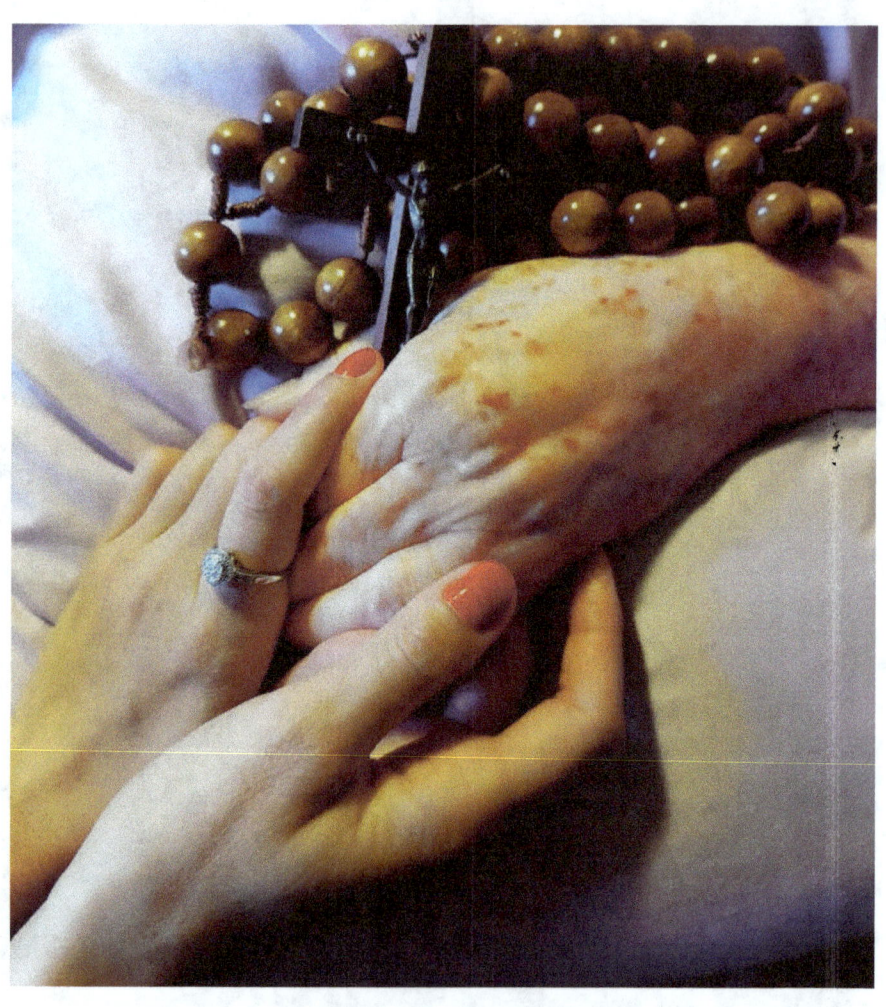

Perhaps the saddest, but sweetest, photo of all, me holding Mami's hand in mine as she passed on from this life. She was at peace, ready to go and was smiling, happy with all she had achieved for us, her children. She gave me that diamond ring of hers to always keep her with me.

Chapter 34:

Cannes Film Festival 2021

*Grief is a process and commitments can help ease the healing—
Blanca Blanco*

Soon after Mami had passed, I was to attend the Cannes Film Festival in France. The heart-breaking part is that I know I will never be able to hold my Mami's hand again and the sense of loss, numbness, and helplessness made me feel so vulnerable. I felt exhausted and drained although I still kept working on my book. It was therapeutic and it gave me the chance to write about my love for Mami now that she was forever gone from our physical world. I also took some "me time" to process my feelings and try to make small day-to-day changes to help myself just get through.

I understood grief would lessen over time but the scar will always be there. With time, we learn how to manage and hopefully enjoy life. I had good and bad days and I knew that was part of the process. I received my talent credentials and the invitation from the Cannes Film Festival to attend in July, but when mom got sick, I canceled it because I wanted to spend all the time with my mom. After mom passed a week later, my aunts and sisters encouraged me to attend the Festival, telling me that it would be good for me instead of just isolating at home and would help with the healing and processing of my loss.

Starting my "firsts" which were my continuing experiences, but now without mom in this world, made me sad because I always called her, to share my experiences with her. She always looked forward to hearing from me about where I was and what I was doing. I agreed to go because I needed to be proactive and going would help with the grieving process, plus it would give me an opportunity for transformation.

I cried during the entire flight, feeling heartbroken, but I knew I would be okay. This in no way diminished my feelings of loss and emptiness but Mom's strong presence was there with me and that gave me strength.

While the 2020 edition had been canceled due to COVID-19, the Cannes Film Festival took place at the Palais des Festival in July 2021. It was great to see so many actors and actresses looking beautiful, especially since this was the first Red Carpet for all of us since the pandemic began. Of course on the Red Carpet, we all wore masks but while getting photographed we were able to take them off just for the picture. Daily testing was done by the festival staff so it felt safe but one always has to take precautions even if we are vaccinated.

Talk about being busy and filling up my time there, I was doing 14 hour days with meetings and interviews, thanks to my team working hard. In the mornings I would walk on the beach to just breathe and be grateful and to help me process what I was going through.

These film festivals are where we can all meet our peers, actors, producers, directors, and everyone associated with the movie industry. I love attending them and I love the energy and excitement the event produces. In fact, I can say that being at these festivals, especially the Cannes Film Festival is very productive, which is just how I like it. The photoshoots and the brilliant films that I enjoyed watching took my mind off things. Although I felt awkward the first time I was back in a theater since the pandemic, thankfully masking up was mandatory and reinforced as the staff was walking back and forth checking on anyone that didn't mask up. Attending this festival, so soon after my mother's passing was just what I needed to "get back on the horse."

While I was away at Cannes my family and I, did a Novena (prayers) for my mom via Zoom every day, for nine days. These sessions were therapeutic and made me feel a sense of comfort to know we are all dealing with the same loss and sharing our experiences helped me with the healing process.

Also while there, and on a more positive thought, I was happy to see Jodie Foster receive Cannes Film Festival's honorary "Palme d'Or" as a lifetime achievement award. She was a special guest at the opening ceremony to collect her award. I have always enjoyed watching her work since I was a young girl and it was great to see that she got that award.

The prize has previously been given to many for their contributions to the movie industry including Agnès Varda and Alain Delon, Jane Fonda, and many more. The award recognizes their artistic career achievement and a commitment to major issues.

John was kind and traveled with me, to Cannes, for emotional support so it felt great not to be alone during the darkest moments of my life. We have been together in good times and bad times.

In one of the Red Carpet appearances, I wore the most beautiful evening gown, designed by Christophe Guillarme, with flowers embroidered around a low cut V neck fitted bodice and a beautiful pink blending to deep salmon skirt with beautifully designed layered rows of pink, to salmon red, crinoline that made the lower part of the gown flare out to the bottom. It was like a colorful Cinderella ball gown. I loved it!

We were there for 12 days. I loved it there, on the French Riviera, with the old buildings and the beautiful unique classy shops with high fashion.

While I was at Cannes, I learned that my latest TV show, *Tale of Tails,* had landed the number 2 spot on Tubi! Great news to hear, especially during my challenging healing process.

I want to share how my trip helped me with the healing process:

- A sense of guilt is there when planning a trip after a loss, treat it as part of a healing process and transformation.

- A trip has an element of reflection both inner and physical, so allow us to reflect on what happened.

- See the beauty around you, be present, and connect with others.

- Traveling served as a positive distraction and helped me start the healing process.

- It does not need to be a trip far away, it could be to the mall, to the beach, around your block, getting nails done, massages, anything that takes you away from isolation.

- Grief can be shifted to a better place.

- Someone told me this after I lost my mom and it really stuck with me. Grief is deep love with nowhere to go since our loved one is not here anymore.

- We all learn to carry our grief differently.

Chapter 35:

Film and Television

Tale of Tails

My most recent role was in *Tale of Tails* a drama, action-thriller TV series. I played "Lola," a young Latina dancer. Lola strives for a better life and is hopeful life will improve for her and her family. In her past, she has made regrettable decisions and ended up working at a low-rent strip club. My role is pivotal to the plot because I hold the key to a crime that can help solve that case. I enjoyed developing my character; a strong female who was vulnerable and who went through a range of emotions, in the situations she found herself in, living her daily life.

I took pole dancing lessons on my own so when I showed up on set, I was fully prepared. I admire the women who can do this for a living it's a hard life.

I read my script over and over until I had my lines memorized and I also understood what was going on in the script and the story. I worked on the specifics and clear choices of each scene; my objectives, my actions, my emotional states, my relationships, and physical activities for that scene. It was long hours of preparation at home on a daily basis, I enjoyed the process of developing my role.

I also improvised while I was offset, each morning, for example, when brushing my hair, I put myself in the shoes of Lola and improvised all day. I invested so many hours in creating this fun character. I knew that hard work pays off, director and producer Harley Wallen was impressed and happy with my work and all the preparation I did before arriving on set and it showed. The show was aired on June 12 on Tubi and was trending well. *Tale of Tails* is now is showing in Italy.

Betrayed

Another role I would like to tell you about was in the movie *Betrayed,* an action-drama thriller. The film is about the many young women who are abducted, drugged, and often found dead. In the movie, a crime is being solved concerning the mayor's daughter. I played "Melanie" the villain of the film. My role was that of a very dark, dramatic character.

My character had a hard past and went through a similar experience as the other girls and she was able to make a business out of it. I enjoyed her range of emotions and the many layers this character offered. Her actions of course were not socially acceptable but as an actor one does not judge the character, although we are committed to developing it.

The character's strength and the mystery were intriguing. I loved how strong and determined this businesswoman was, successful yet vulnerable, with a hard past who was emotionally driven with so much mystery behind her character.

Once again, I prepared my character for a couple of months before filming and worked on my script for hours working on my role. It was a good set to work on and my scenes were so emotional that when I was playing them, I often made those present on set cry, and in some of my scenes they were also scared. That is a good indication that my interpretation of the character was on target. I have to say, as actors, it feels good when the producers and the director are happy with our work.

My role was recognized and I won *Best Supporting Actress* in a film festival. I was so humbled and honored. It was actually the first award I had ever won in my acting career and it felt so good.

The film was shot in Detroit and sadly the story is based on true events. When studying for this role I researched into the entire kidnapping and sex trade horror that is going on, not only here in this country and back in Mexico, but all over the world. So, when I was playing the role, it was very real to me. I wanted to portray her because I was representing a real-life person. It was very important to me that all those watching the movie believed in the character I played.

I was very honored that Harley Wallen, Director/Producer of *Tale of Tails* and *Betrayed* wrote the following kind note about working with me.

Harley Wallen, Painted Creek Productions[3]

It was interesting how I even came to find out about Blanca for my film Betrayed back in 2017. My friend Ray Morgis had worked with her previously and thought she had great screen presence and knows how important that is to me so I looked her up and I was excited to see a good sense of truth in her craft as well as the screen presence Ray had mentioned.

After talking about her role, I was also excited to see her taking it serious enough to do the work needed coming to Michigan to shoot, needing very little direction on set. I had a really strong ensemble cast for this very important human trafficking film and Blanca really researched her role and gave really good depth and dimension to her performance. It was great to see her win Best Actress Award for her work as "Melanie" in Betrayed and well deserved in my opinion!

I recently had an opportunity to work with her again in 2020, this time taking on a very different role as a guest star on my first season of the multi-award-winning TV show Tale of Tails. This time she portrayed "Lola," a dancer at a "blue-collar strip club".

*These types of roles can be tricky to perform, especially knowing you have to remove your mind's "third eye" and not be self-conscious as you are for the most part not wearing much. What really struck me the second time working with Blanca was her commitment to her craft and although she was fantastic to work with, the first time around the work she had put into herself was much more than noticeable. I consider Blanca to be a bit of an industry secret when it comes to a high-quality actress with the ability to **play a variety of roles at a high***

---

[3] https://www.imdb.com/name/nm6136445/

level with fantastic screen presence, strong truth in performance and it doesn't hurt she's got a nice following!

On a personal note, from spending time working together with her. I feel privileged to call her a friend and look forward to many more collaborations in the future. With all her beauty and talent, she still somehow has remained a really good person that's an absolute joy to be around.

Chapter 36:

Paris, Je T'Aime

Paris is a land of great beauty and history. — Blanca Blanco

I was now doing fashion editorials as well as my acting career and the two were entirely different, but they worked well together. I was photographed many times as I progressed in both of my careers I began to appear as an item in fashion magazines. When I attended Red Carpet events like the Oscars and the Golden Globes, most of the time, I would go viral and trending which was a humbling experience for me. This led me to be featured in magazines; *Vogue, People, Cosmopolitan, US Weekly, Grazia, Elle, Harper's Bazaar, Gala, Glamour, Forbes, Daily Mail,* and being featured *on Fox News* and so on.

For *Elle,* I became the "Face" for a Swedish brand called Chiquelle. For 2 years, I was frequently featured in *Elle* several times a year. In one year, I was published 3 times in *Elle* magazine, which was amazing for me.

This led to my work with international high-end couture designers. I continue to work with them but with the COVID-19 pandemic, we had to place everything on hold, like everyone else in the world. They usually send their photographer here to the U.S. to do the shoots.

I love doing fashion editorials it's exciting to be photographed by some of the world's best photographers and in locations all over the world. I get to travel to places for work like Paris, London, Rome, Moscow, and Marrakesh. These were places that, as a girl growing up, I never imagined I would ever get to visit. Also as an actress, I get to travel all over the USA and so far, have done films in Monaco and Italy. I love what I do!

Chapter 37:

My Friend, Christophe Guillarme

A true friendship is a journey without an end. — Blanca Blanco

I have open and closed top shows during the *Paris Fashion Week* for coveted Paris fashion designers like Christophe Guillarme whose designer line I represented. It was through one of my photographer friends, that we became good friends and I ended up representing his exclusive line of high fashion designer clothing. I love his designs!

Christophe is now a good friend and often asks me to model his latest designs which I love to do. Now he has my measurements he can make his beautiful and unique designs for me to wear before I even arrive in Paris. Whenever I need a beautiful designer dress, Christophe is always able to provide me with one. I also get to keep a few of these beautiful dresses.

Christophe and I also do a number of editorials throughout the year together. It has been fun working on artistic projects with him and we are very similar in so many ways. For example, we both work very hard and we understand the importance of media placements.

The French media loved what I did and were very kind to me. They covered all I did in Paris with their ability to get me into French fashion magazines and I was always grateful for their help and support and as a result, I had major placements.

Even at my first Oscar appearance, I had become known and I heard my name being called out by photographers looking for a shot, which I always tried to accommodate for them. I thought, wow, they know me, which was one of my goals to become more widely known, and that starts with the photographers. Everyone's role is important and we are interwoven. It is a team effort when one goes viral, but not purely for the fame, although this is flattering, it also allows me to do more, using my name, to help others.

I learned how to walk on the Paris fashion runway (without tripping up) while wearing the long evening gowns. I was now modeling some very expensive designer clothes. When I arrived in Paris, London, or Rome, the Paparazzi were always there to greet me. They were photographing me the entire time so I had to dress well and make sure my makeup and hair were done despite the long flight from the U.S. But I always thought to myself, this is what you do Blanca, embrace and enjoy the moment because it can so quickly pass.

The photographers and paparazzi liked me and I made sure I treated them with respect. After all, they were only doing their jobs trying to earn a living and I knew all about that! They sold my photos to magazines and I appreciated their photography, as it helped us both.

The work involved in Paris fashion week was incredible. I was now collaborating and working with models from all over the world. I had seen many of them in well-known magazines, featured, as I was being featured now in *Elle* and *Vogue*.

My name is out there now in the fashion world and many up-and-coming or new models write to me and ask me for tips and tricks to help them. Apart from make-up and fashion tips, I always respond and tell them to keep in touch with photographers, editors, and others. I tell them what you put in will eventually pay off. Just be consistent in what you do.

My heart was touched when reading this lovely message from my dear friend, Christophe regarding working with me.

Fashion Designer, Christophe Guillarme[4]

Meeting with Blanca at Cannes film Festival in 2018 was really the beginning of a great and genuine friendship! We are both workaholics and it's so empowering to climb the steps of success together, in entertainment for her and fashion for me. During our collaborations, we were lucky to visit amazing destinations, shoot in the most magic of locations. Both of us stayed focused right to the end of each photoshoot to get the job done, with respect of each other's ideas and creativity. It's a real dialogue that we started and I feel blessed to be part of this book and to know that our relationship is as precious for her as she is for me!

---

[4] https://www.christopheguillarme.fr/en/

Chapter 38:

Breaking the Mold Summary

Go confidently in the direction of your dreams! Live the life you've imagined. — Henry David Thoreau

I wanted to write both a motivational and a helpful book based on my own life's challenging experiences, applying the education I received through earning my degrees. They did in fact give me the tools I would need to help me cope with all that was thrown my way, and there were a lot. My childhood experiences shaped me, helped to provide me with remarkable resilience and I learned strategies to overcome these numerous challenges. I also wanted to write a book to inspire people, and to recognize that barriers are merely challenges, that lead to achievable goals. We have that control.

I wanted also to share what I have experienced personally and in doing so be transparent about how I felt and the emotional rollercoaster of my past life. I wrote my book during the devastating COVID-19 pandemic and subsequent lockdown, which gave me motivation and the time to write about all that I have been through and have now shared with you within these pages.

I have told the truth in my stories, about my heartbreaking and challenging childhood memories, experiencing life while living in severe poverty, overcoming language and cultural barriers, which gave me the motivation I needed to succeed. Despite this, I worked through these challenges using day by day, positive "self-talk," treating my problems as mere challenges to be overcome, if I wanted to succeed. So, as a result, I felt a sense of control while I was working on each situation and this, for me, was important.

My childhood experience shaped me into who I am today and equipped me with the many skills I would need to manage life's challenging lessons. The Woolsey Fire became a defining challenge and it took me through the dreadful stages of loss and grief I encountered and had to overcome. Even writing about it, was difficult for me.

I incorporated my psychology background and I have shared the tools I used to help my readers to deal with anxiety or with panic, should you experience this. I shared my personal experiences and hopefully, in doing so, I have helped my readers. My book is about personal growth. It is about taking ownership of our actions and behavior. We are, after all, our own drivers in each of our lives, and knowing this means we each have the ability to become successful. I certainly did!

I have shared how I turned my life around, from poverty to success; earning my master's degree, and working as an actress and model, were each part of my dream to become successful. I defeated the odds and I shared what tools worked for me. I encourage you to try using these tools for yourself.

My fans and my readers will learn about me; the child who became a woman and the woman who became a success. I never had the opportunity, to share many of my life's challenges and my stories that

I believe are perhaps relatable for many who will read my book, until now.

It has become even more important, for me to share all that I learned, especially now during the pandemic, since poverty and abuse have sadly tripled.

I dedicate this book to my sweet Mami who was the one who has inspired me since childhood and who encouraged me to write about all I encountered and to share it here, in the pages of my life.

I also told of how my mom took her terminal diagnosis with so much dignity and bravery despite it happening to her at such a young age. I shared also, how we honored Mami's last wishes to transition from this life, at home and how our family worked as a team to fill her with loving memories in her last days. As I went through the process of grief, it provided comfort knowing my family and I are all grieving together and we continue to support each other during this journey of grief. Grief is a lifetime process because one never stops loving that person who is now gone from our lives but one learns to carry this weight differently or at least we learn to manage it.

Just two weeks after mom's passing, I was committed to attending the Cannes Film Festival, in the South of France, followed by the Magna Graecia Film Festival, in Calabria, Italy. Although I was heartbroken, because it finally hit me about the reality of Mami not being here and feeling numb I followed through with my commitments while still feeling vulnerable and emotionally uncertain that I could fulfill them. Life continues and one has to take steps forward, taking it one day at a time.

While I was sharing thoughts and stories in this book, I discovered new self-insights and self-discovery; things about me that helped my healing process, things that I didn't know I possessed. I learned that grieving could last for a lifetime and I also learned to manage my life and that helped my healing process. I learned to take back control of my life and why getting back on the horse was so important. Someone told me grief is just love with nowhere to go because the person is not here, but remembering them keeps them with us and, for me, was part of being able to cope.

In coming to the end of my book I sincerely hope that you were motivated to understand that anyone can face their own difficulties and overcome them. In doing so, one learns how important drive and determination are in completing our goals if we choose to set our goals rather than just allowing time to pass us by while doing nothing.

I truly believe we are the ones to control our own destiny, not others. So if nothing else, try to let the bad things from the past go and think of the positive things you would love to do in your future. Use the past experiences as things you can learn from to manage your personal success as I had to do.

I wanted to show you, at the end of my book, the successful me, the "me now" as a contrast to all the trauma and all the difficulties that I encountered in my past; poverty, an unsupportive father, the Woolsey Fire, and how I felt about these things as they happened.

I am living a life I never thought was possible. I made it happen through determination, education, and a burning ambition to change my life's trajectory and break the mold.

My message to everyone is this. There is no magic in making success happen for yourself, but you have to take that first step, whatever that first step is for you. Taking that first step towards your goal is key, make plans to change what you can change, and don't worry about the things you can't change.

I found that consistency, tenacity, and hard work, staying on course, and patience were the keys to reaching my success. After reading my book I ask that you call your mom or your family members, just to say "hi" or better still, to say "I love you" or, "I was just thinking about you," as love is the strongest and most powerful emotion in the entire universe.

I hope that you can take away from reading my book that one can go through traumas and come out as a survivor and still thrive in life. *Breaking the Mold* is my life story of personal victory and sheer determination of defying the statistical odds stacked against me.

If I have inspired just one person, then I achieved my goal because that person can inspire another and the next and so on creating a tsunami and a domino effect, how cool would that be!

My final message to you all is, BE KIND, RESPECT OTHERS, SHARE YOUR LOVE, AND LIVE FOR TODAY! I have enjoyed writing my book and sharing it with you all and I hope you have enjoyed reading it.

With much love from me, Blanca Blanco. I'll see you all at the movies!

Stay safe, get COVID-19 tested, and please wear a mask!

Chapter 39:

Movies and TV Shows

A collage of several roles I have played in different films including *Betrayed, Tale of Tails* and *Ember,* where I was made to look bald, the magic of the silver screen.

Tale of Tails, "Lola"

Betrayed, filmed in Detroit. I played "Melanie"
I won the award for Best Supporting Actress.

Eye for Eye, filmed in Montana USA.
It was a period 1800's western, shot in 2021. I played the
lead role as "Lola."

Chapter 40:

Photos, Editorials, and Interviews

Photoshoot in Los Angeles
Photo by Filip Shobot

Photoshoot in Los Angeles
Photo by Filip Shobot

Chiquelle editorial for Elle magazine, Serbian
edition, location Los Angeles, December 2018
photo by Filip Shobot

Headshot photoshoot in Los Angeles
Photo by Filip Shobot

Photoshoot in downtown Los Angeles
Photo by Filip Shobot

Photoshoot in Los Angeles
Photo by Filip Shobot

251

Photoshoot in Los Angeles
Photo by Filip Shobot

Photoshoot in Los Angeles,
for Elle magazine, June 2019
Photo by Filip Shobot

Chiquelle editorial for Elle magazine for their
Serbian Edition.
Location Malibu CA
Photo by Filip Shobot

Photoshoot for Elle magazine August 2019

Photo by Filip Shobot

Story Magazine "Beauty" editorial
Photo by Filip Shobot

Black and white photoshoot
Photo by Filip Shobot

Black and white headshot
Photo by Filip Shobot

Photoshoot for Hola magazine, Marrakesh Morocco
Photo and gown by Christophe Guillarme

Interview for Grazia Maroc magazine, wearing
Christopher Guillarme   Location-Marrakech Morocco
Photo credit- Christophe Guillarme

Photoshoot in Black and White
Photo by Filip Shobot

Photoshoot for Hola magazine interview and editorial, location Marrakesh, Morocco, I am wearing Christophe Guillarme.
Photo by Christophe Guillarme

Me with my friend, the incredibly
talented, French fashion designer
Christophe Guillarme

Chapter 41:

In the Limelight:

On the Red Carpet

The Oscars Red Carpet, Los Angeles at the
Kodak Theater — I designed the dress.

The Latin Grammy's, Red Carpet, Las Vegas
Nevada, one week after the Woolsey Fire.
Wearing Christophe Guillarme.

The Oscars, Red Carpet wearing Quynh Paris

Cannes Film Festival, Red Carpet, viral looks.
Wearing Christophe Guillarme. The green dress is
Sahar Saleh Couture.

Magna Graecia Film Festival, Red Carpet

Catanzaro, Italy

The Golden Globes in Los Angeles.

Wearing Christophe Guillarme.

The yellow gown I designed.
Photo Filip Shobot

Chapter 42:
Film and TV Roles

2021	Eye for Eye	Lola
2021	Tale of Tails	Lola
2019	Hold On	Luna
2018	Betrayed	Melanie
2018	Woman on the Edge	Natalie
2018	Ovid and the Art of Love	Alamenia
2018	Six Children and One Grandfather	Matilda
2018	Mission Possible	Lillian
2018	Followed	Nic's Stepmom
2018	The Dog of Christmas	Jennifer
2017	Torch	Rolanda Monero
2017	Spreading Darkness	Vera
2017	Fake News	Lupita
2016	Teen Star Academy	Julia
2016	Fishes 'n Loaves : Heaven Sent	Judine
2016	American Romance	Miranda
2015	The Sparrows: Nesting	Blair
2015	Beverly Hills Christmas	Delia
2015	Sensory Perception	Senator Magdalena
2014	Bullet	Maria Espinoza
2014	Bermuda Tentacles (TV Movie)	Natalie
2014	Crimes of the Mind (TV Movie)	The Guardian
2014	Whitney (TV Movie)	Agent Lopez
2014	On Air (TV Movie)	Serena
2013	Awakened	Mrs. Foster
2013	Defending Santa	Ana
2013	Discarded	Nurse Blanca
2011	Showgirls 2: Penny's from Heaven	Mrs. Von Brausen
2010	The Last Chicana	Blanca
2008	Dark Reel	Claudia

Reference 1:

Abuse and Moving Forward

For anyone who has experienced any type of abuse, it is important to remember that your past does not define you, and is not your fault, as you can see with my story, I have used my experiences to propel me forward in my journey. I hope that my book can inspire you to put light into the darkness of any repressed memories to heal those wounds. Trauma will weigh us down, making it harder to grow as a person, and experience life to the fullest. Let's be kind with ourselves, take small steps forward. Positive affirmations are a powerful tool to help us recondition our mind, and thought processes.

* * * * *

Relaxation Techniques

I will share some of the tools I use when dealing with my anxiety that are effective for me and I am confident they can work for you, too. I work on relaxation and breathing techniques like **Deep Breathing** morning and night for about 3-5 minutes. Breathing exercises helped with my anxiety and stress. Taking a deep breath, *breathing in and breathing out*, helps one to stay centered and become relaxed. Did you know a deep breath is the one thing that travels and touches most organs in our bodies?

I also practice **Mindfulness Meditation** focusing on breathing. The primary focus is to remind me to keep my mind in the present moment. That's the challenge because thoughts seem to race or speed to the future and one has to work on redirecting their thoughts to the present because the goal is to stay In the NOW.

Another great way that I worked on relaxing was using the **Body Scan Technique,** which I use, especially when I was driving to escape the Woolsey Fire. I would start with deep breathing and the second part would be to focus on a body part. By focusing on a body part and breathing in, help release tension, and the heaviness of the anxiety feels lighter and lighter. Leaving my body feeling more relaxed.

* * * * *

Body Shaming is Bullying

I mentioned earlier that I would get bullied at school and sometimes at home, body shaming is real and it is not okay. I experienced body shaming during middle and high school and even at times now in the entertainment industry. Body shaming is criticizing, judging, or making negative comments about someone's weight such as "too skinny" "too fat" and so on. I was told I was too skinny, too bony, not curvy enough, my legs were too long, my eyebrows were too bushy, my waist was too small, and the list went on. Body shaming is linked to depression and anxiety and I remember how hurtful it was as a child. When I was a teenager, I even asked my doctor if he could prescribe me medication to gain weight because I started believing there was something wrong.

Luckily with time and working on my positive self-image and re-framing, I was able to recognize that when people criticize others, they are usually projecting their own insecurities on you to make themselves feel better about their own issues. I learned to ignore them and focus instead on self-love and being kinder with myself. I decided that if I was going to change anything about my body, it would be for me. It wouldn't be for external validation. I had to take responsibility and ownership by saying YES to accept my body and to be proud of it. With time, I became more comfortable wearing bikinis and decided not to hide, but to own it!

I focused on health, self-love and ignored trolls. In the entertainment industry, one is analyzed like a science experiment, much like being in a petri dish, with trolls criticizing every inch of our bodies. However, my childhood experience shaped me and prepared me, and as a result, gave me personal growth and acceptance.

Remember those that bully feel powerless and they suffer from insecurities. When they focus on YOU, it makes them feel better. You are exactly who they wish they were. Not to mention one must be grateful for their health, as that's a privilege some people do not have.

Remember, it is YOUR body, don't let trolls dictate your happiness. It all starts with YOU.

Reference 2:

Poverty Affecting Children

Part of my degree was focused on how poverty affects children, something I knew a lot about firsthand. I was interested to see what drove the continuation of child poverty into future generations when it need not be the case. This is part of the paper I wrote for my degree at Eastern Washington University.

Childhood mortality has decreased since 1980, because of the various public assistance programs. The program, "Aid to families with dependent children (AFDC) was the biggest public assistance. The objective of the child welfare was to assist the families who were in need.

There are several problems affecting children because of poverty. The data shows poverty is influencing child psychological development and academic performance because of financial stress. Furthermore, a correlation between academic performance and poverty shows it is affecting child development.

In 2001, the poverty rate in children was 11.7 million, however, this increased to 12.1 in the year 2002. Children who are living in a family with only a female provider, no male present, are 48.6 percent in poverty.

In 1990, The World Summit for Children organization was established because of the Child Survival Revolution of 1980. The objective was to decrease the child mortality by a third. The obtained data showed today 63% of child deaths could be prevented with interventions programs.

Poor children are more likely to suffer from psychological problems and academic achievement as well. Research showed children who are not suffering from poverty were somewhat less likely to suffer from mental health problems than poor children were.

A home anchors a family in the community and provides children with the stability they need to develop and grow, furthermore, studies have found that even a moderate amount of under-nutrition has a lasting effect on children's development and school performance as well.

In addition, data indicated children's health contributes to the development of mental health depression tendencies in children. It was found that hunger links to depression, academic and psychological development of children. Likewise, children who lived in an environment (home) with hunger and have enough food, are less likely to have failed a grade and to have lower math scores.

Because of poverty affecting children's development, there was a law established in order to alleviate child poverty. designed to promote healthy development of children, President Theodore Roosevelt initiated the White House Conference on Children and Youth, as he perceived poverty as an issue affecting the children.

The effect of the child welfare program was to provide assistance to families who were in need. There was a strategy to keep mothers at home. Furthermore, the AFDC was very effective.

Throughout history, numerous programs had developed in order to fulfill individual needs including children. There is a correlation between poverty and health effect in children. The children are our future; thus the development of the children is essential for the future.

References:

Lang, S., Susan (2002). *Hunger and Poverty in children is linked to depression and low achievement*

Lurie, L., Harry (1999) Encyclopedia of Social Work: *Child Welfare*, 15, 137-144).

McLeod, D., Jane & Shanahan, J., Michael, (1996*). Trajectories of Poverty and Children's Mental Health*, Journal of health and social behavior. 207-211

Proctor, D., Bernadette & Draker, Joseph (2003) *Poverty in the United States 2002*. United States Department of Commerce, 2-7.

Worner Van, Katherine. (2003). *Social Welfare:* A World View (pp72-77). United States Thompson Custom Publishing Co.

Reference 3:

Dealing with Panic Attacks

Panic attacks are sudden, intense surges of fear, panic, or anxiety. They are overwhelming and they have physical as well as emotional symptoms. I have had only 2 panic attacks.

Many people with panic attacks may have difficulty breathing, sweat profusely, tremble and feel their hearts pounding. A few people will also experience chest pain and a feeling of detachment from reality or themselves during a panic attack, so they may think they're having a heart attack. Others have reported feeling like they are having a stroke.

Panic attacks can be scary and may hit you quickly. Here are 11 strategies you can use to try to stop a panic attack when you're having one or when you feel one coming on:

Use Deep Breathing

If you're able to control your breathing, you're less likely to experience the hyperventilating that can make other symptoms, and the panic attack itself, worse. Focus on taking deep breaths and breathe in for a count of four, hold for a second and then breathe out for a count of four.

Recognize That You're Having a Panic Attack

Recognizing that you're having a panic attack instead of a heart attack, is temporary, it will pass. Take away the fear that you may be dying. This can allow you to focus on other techniques to reduce your symptoms.

Close Your Eyes

Triggers can overwhelm you. If you're in a fast-paced environment close your eyes during your panic attack. This can block out any extra stimuli and make it easier to focus on your breathing.

Practice Mindfulness

Focus on the physical sensations you are familiar with, like digging your feet into the ground or feeling the texture of your jeans on your hands. These specific sensations ground you firmly in reality and give you something objective to focus on.

Find a Focus Object

Pick one object in clear sight and consciously note everything about it possible. For example, you may notice how the hand on the clock jerks when it ticks and that it's slightly lopsided. Describe the patterns, color, shapes, and size of the object to yourself. Focus all of your energy on this object and your panic symptoms may subside.

Use Muscle Relaxation Techniques

Much like deep breathing, muscle relaxation techniques can help stop your panic attack in its tracks by controlling your body's response as much as possible. Consciously relax one muscle at a time, starting with something simple like the fingers in your hand and move your way up through your body.

Picture Your Happy Place

What's the most relaxing place in the world that you can think of? A sunny beach with gently rolling waves? A cabin in the mountains? Picture yourself there and try to focus on the details as much as possible. Imagine digging your toes into the warm sand or smelling the sharp scent of pine trees. This place should be quiet, calm, and relaxing.

Engage in Light Exercise

Endorphins keep the blood pumping in exactly the right way. Because you're stressed, choose light exercise that's gentle on the body, like walking or swimming.

Keep Lavender on Hand

Lavender is known for being soothing and stress-relieving. It can help your body relax. If you know you're prone to panic attacks, keep some lavender essential oil on hand and put some on your forearms when you experience a panic attack. Breathe in the scent.

Repeat a Mantra Internally

Repeating a mantra internally can be relaxing and reassuring and it can give you something to grasp onto during a panic attack.

References:

Healthline, medically reviewed by Timothy J. Legg, Ph.D., CRNP — Written by Ana Gotter — Updated on December 7, 2018. "Panic attacks."

Reference 4:

Dealing With Grief

Processing Grief

In 1969, psychiatrist Elisabeth Kübler-Ross introduced what became known as the "five stages of grief." These stages of grief were based on her studies based on the feelings of patients facing terminal illness, but many people have generalized them to other types of negative life changes and losses, such as the death of a loved one or a break-up. However, the journey through dealing with grief is not linear and not necessarily experienced in the order shown below.

The Journey of working through grief:

1. **Denial:** "This can't be happening to me."

2. **Anger:** "Why is this happening?" "Who is to blame?"

3. **Bargaining:** "Make this not happen and in return, I will _____."

4. **Depression:** "I'm too sad to do anything."

5. **Acceptance:** Acceptance does not mean that the person feels good or right about the loss. Most people never feel OK about the loss of a loved one or their own impending death. This stage is about accepting the fact that a new reality cannot be changed. It is about seeing how the new reality will impact life and relationships.[5]

---

[5] https://www.econdolence.com/

If you are experiencing any of these emotions following a loss, it may help to know that your reaction is natural and that you will heal in time. Contrary to popular belief, you do not have to go through each of the above to heal. In fact, some people resolve their grief without going through any of these processes for managing grief. But we are all different, aren't we?

Kübler-Ross herself never intended for "these stages" to be a rigid framework that applies to everyone who mourns. Our grieving is as individual as our lives.

Grief Can Be a Roller Coaster

We might also think of the grieving process as a roller coaster, full of ups and downs, highs and lows. Like many roller coasters, the ride tends to be rougher in the beginning, the lows may be deeper and longer. The difficult periods should become less intense and shorter as time goes by, but it takes time to work through a loss. Even years after a loss, especially at special events such as a family wedding or the birth of a child, we may still experience a strong sense of grief.

For more information, go to the Source: Hospice Foundation of America

Biography

Blanca Blanco is an American actress who was born in Watsonville, California. While still very young, her family moved back to Mexico. At the age of nine, her family relocated to Chelan, Washington, where she began taking acting and singing classes and organizing theatre performances in between her studies. She has two sisters and two brothers.

After high school, Blanca attended Washington State University where she graduated with a Bachelor of Science degree in Psychology. From there she went on to earn a master's degree in social work from Eastern Washington University. All of her degrees were completed with honors.

After relocating to Los Angeles to pursue a career in acting, she began training under DGA Award-winning director Gordon Hunt. Additionally, Blanca enrolled in UCLA's acting program as well as The groundlings. Blanca still trains weekly with Academy Award nominee Sally Kirkland and veteran character actor Bruce Glover.

Her first major role was in the 2008 feature film *Dark Reel,* opposite Edward Furlong. She can also be seen in *Anatomy of Deception* (Lifetime), *Crimes of the Mind* (Lifetime), *Defending Santa* (ION), and *Bermuda Tentacles* (Syfy). Notable on-screen credits include *Torch* opposite Rita Moreno, *Fake news* opposite Eric Roberts, *6 Children & 1 Grandparent* opposite Oscar nominee Burt Young,

Woman on the Edge, opposite Rumer Willis, *Hold On* opposite Luis Guzmán, *American Romance* opposite Nolan Gerard Funk.

In her recently released film *Betrayed,* she won Best Supporting Actress for her villain role at the International Independent Film Festival distributed by Sony. Blanca's latest TV series *Tale of Tails,* released on Tubi, is doing very well. Her work on this project has been recognized, and Season 2 is in the works.

Blanca is a supporter of the L.A. Mission, American Cancer Society, Autism Speaks, The Salvation Army, Step Up, and has worked as a counselor for End of Life hospice patients.

Blanca Blanco has completed her first book, *Breaking the Mold* (Briton Publishing), winning the "Favorite Inspirational Book" literary award from the Hollywood Global Film Festival. Blanca currently resides in Beverly Hills, CA.

www.ingramcontent.com/pod-product-compliance
Lightning Source LLC
Chambersburg PA
CBHW061139120626
46546CB00005B/1855